SABELO MLANGENI

The Tate Photography Series is a celebration of international and British photography in the Tate collection and an introduction to some of the most significant photographers at work today.

Each book focuses on an individual photographer and features a specially selected sequence of photographs, an introduction by a Tate curator, and a conversation with the photographer. These collaborations between living artists and experts enrich our understanding of photography and its connection to everyday life, and move from city streets to seashores, across landscapes and subcultures, through identities and interiors, in a visual travelogue of our world today.

Set against the various social, political and cultural issues of our time, the theme for Series One is Community and Solidarity, which brings together four photographers, unrelated as individual artists yet unified here by their work. A Ghanaian-Russian photographer joins Black Lives Matter street protests in London, an artist-activist in New Delhi chronicles women's emancipatory struggles, a South-African's camera locates queer lives in rural townships, while a Finnish-British photographer captures the community spirit in the North-East of England as perhaps only an émigré can.

Work from several continents is brought together, connected by shared practice. In all of these locations and environments, each imbued with unique struggles and dangers, a commonality of human character and strength inspired by community and solidarity is portrayed, permitting glimpses of joy and hope.

Series One

1:1   **LIZ JOHNSON ARTUR**
1:2   **SIRKKA-LIISA KONTTINEN**
1:3   **SABELO MLANGENI**
1:4   **SHEBA CHHACHHI**

SABELO MLANGENI

Edited by
Sarah Allen

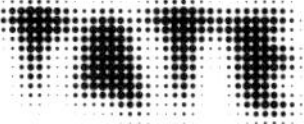

First published 2022 by order of the Tate Trustees
by Tate Publishing, a division of Tate Enterprises Ltd,
Millbank, London SW1P 4RG
www.tate.org.uk/publishing

A catalogue record for this book is available from
the British Library
ISBN 978 1 84976 802 3

Distributed in the United States and Canada
by ABRAMS, New York

Library of Congress Control Number applied for

Series Editors: Simon Armstrong and Yasufumi
Nakamori
Senior Editor: Nicola Bion
Production: Bill Jones
Picture Research: Emma O'Neill
Designed by Sarah Boris
Colour reproduction by Westerham Press, London
Printed and bound in the UK by Westerham Press,
London

Front cover: *A morning after Umlindelo* 2016
(from the series *Umlindelo wamaKholwa*)
Back cover: (top) *Olalere's body painting shoot
(make up artist Thom Smith and Daniel)* 2019
(from the series *The Royal House of Allure*); (bottom)
Room mates 2008 (from the series *Men Only*)

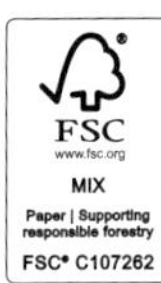

CONTENTS

INTRODUCTION

Sabelo Mlangeni tells stories of communities who inhabit spaces often on the periphery of society. Time plays an important role in the process: Mlangeni invests extended periods of time in building relationships, gaining trust and, eventually, access to inner circles and sacred spaces.

Born in 1980 in a rural area of Driefontein near Wakkerstroom outside Johannesburg, one of Mlangeni's first jobs was assisting a local photographer, Mrs C.S. Mavuso – cleaning her studio, running deliveries and collecting payments. Photography chose him in a sense as, one day, armed with a camera and a crash course in photography, he was tasked by Mrs Mavuso with shooting a local couple's wedding. Mlangeni never actually saw the images he had taken that day, but it was the experience of working for, and within, a community that sparked a desire to continue making images.

In 2001, aged twenty-one, he moved to Johannesburg – a city once described by writer Bongani Madondo as 'an economic hub, behemoth African bazaar, the nexus at which an exploding continental otherworldliness and a saturation of pan-African pavement capitalism smooch first world architecture ... a city thinly held together by the ethos of convenience and active, almost punk-like dissonance.'[1] Swapping rural life for Johannesburg delivered a lightning bolt shock to Mlangeni's system.

Survival in the big city is often about finding your people, and shortly after arriving he found a home at Market Photo Workshop. It was a pivotal moment. Market Photo Workshop holds a special place in the history of photography in South Africa: it was founded by the photographer David Goldblatt as a space for Black photographers to learn photography and access workshops, education and international photographers. Today it counts many world-renowned photographers amongst its alumni.

Mlangeni's first series *Big City* (2002–15) focused on Johannesburg's constant state of architectural renewal. But for Mlangeni his interest in the city always exists in dialogue with its relationship to the rural. His following series *At Home* (2004–9) documented rural areas surrounding his hometown of Driefontein and his series *Ghost Town* (2009–11) shows country towns that 'freedom and opportunity have somehow skipped past'.[2] Although not always front and centre in these particular series, people are at the heart of Mlangeni's photography, often those who have been pushed to the so-called 'margins', or whose stories could have easily gone untold.

In 2006 Mlangeni began photographing women who sweep the streets of Johannesburg at night. The project was prompted by the realisation that he had never stopped to consider how Johannesburg's streets, piled high with rubbish by sundown, were clean by break of day. The artist spent eight months getting to know the street sweepers, the women he calls 'mothers of the city'. Some evenings he left his camera at home, choosing instead to sweep by their side. The series that resulted, *Invisible Women* (2006) includes heroic portraits of women posing proudly displaying the tools of their trade. It also shows the women at work - their sweeping frozen by the camera in a painterly swoop, a nightly labour rendered as if it were some beautiful ballet.

An exploration of gender roles has become a career-long interest for Mlangeni, and in *Men Only* (2008–9) he was drawn to the George Goch Hostel on the East Rand of Johannesburg. The hostel only permits male residents, many of whom have moved to Johannesburg seeking out better opportunities. Mlangeni photographed outside the hostel for almost two years before he was invited in. Stereotypes shroud such spaces, yet his images challenge our expectations by showing glimpsed moments of tenderness and intimacy.

In his exploration of gender and sexuality Mlangeni is one of a generation of photographers who are seeking a new visuality for South African photography beyond the era of 'struggle photography'.[3] He was fourteen when apartheid ended and so came of age at a time when a young Republic was taking its first tentative steps. Yet that is not to say the spectre of apartheid doesn't linger within the work. Stark divisions between racially segregated communities are evident. In *My Storie* (2012) Mlangeni photographed white residents in the suburb of Bertrams, Johannesburg. In *No Problem* (2013) the artist documented the Alexandra township, contrasting it with the neighbouring Sandton, a wealthy and predominantly white suburb which in the 1990s became a business centre and synonymous with 'white flight'.

South Africa's new democracy ushered in one of the most progressive constitutions in the world – it was the first to outlaw discrimination based on sexual orientation. The birth of the Rainbow Nation saw increased visibility for many forms of Black queer self-expression. Between 2003 and 2009, Mlangeni photographed queer communities in rural areas of the Mpumalanga province where he grew up. He photographed across Driefontein, Ermelo, Bethal, Platrand, Piet Retief, Standerton and Secunda, capturing individuals, many of whom prefer to be called 'Girls'. In his series *Country Girls* (2003–9) formally posed, glamorous portraits are interspersed with images of parties, pageants and quiet moments of everyday life at home.

Whereas queer life in the city has long drawn the lens of photographers, LGBTQIA+ lives in the countryside are far less visualised. And though we might presume that the rural context might be more hostile, associated as it often is with conservatism and tradition, the situation is more complex. The scholar Graeme Reid points out that the queer community brings the very latest fashion to the countryside which plays to the rural 'desire for the new': 'modernity is at once threatening and desirable, and to the extent that gays occupy this symbolic space, they are both celebrated and despised.'[14]

Despite South Africa's constitution, which enshrines LGBTQIA+ rights, homophobia and hate crimes are widespread. Yet Mlangeni's work seeks to recentre themes of friendship, love and joy in the face of ever-present risk. This was again the case when he travelled to Lagos, Nigeria to work with the residents of the Royal House of Allure. House-ballroom communities date back to nineteenth-century New York, and over the decades evolved into safe spaces specifically for Black and Latino gay and queer individuals. In Nigeria same-sex relations are criminalised and punishable by a jail term. The Royal House of Allure is therefore a refuge but also a space for radical queer self-expression, solidarity and, a family that you choose.

Another family that Mlangeni has photographed is one very close to his heart – the family of worshippers in his own Zionist Christian church. Zionism is the largest religious movement in South Africa. During the colonial period, it grew in popularity because of the discriminatory policies of the mission churches. Mlangeni has been a member of the church since childhood; his images capture the community and its rituals as well as Zionism's deep connection to the land as a faith that exists without church buildings, instead worshipping in open air.

Mlangeni's photography of the Zionist church includes an image from 1997, the first year he took a photograph, and images made as recently as 2021. This fact illustrates his interest in a continued engagement, one in which he often returns to photograph his subject anew, always with a keen awareness that the deepest collaborations are earned over time. Above all, Mlangeni's images tell stories of seeking out your people, choosing a family and building a home, wherever you find yourself.

Sarah Allen
Head of Programme, South London Gallery

1   Bongani Madondo, 'Big City', *Aperture*, Summer 2017, p.56, archive.aperture.org/article/2017/2/2/sabelo-mlangeni-big-city, accessed 26 Oct. 2021. 2

2   Sabelo Mlangeni, 'Ghost Towns', archive.stevenson.info/exhibitions/mlangeni/index2011.html, accessed 26 Oct. 2021.

3   Resistance or struggle photography is a term describing the photographic documentation of conflict between oppressed and oppressor from the perspective of the subjugated. 'Politics and Photography in Apartheid South Africa', David L. Krantz, *History of Photography*, Vol.32, 2008, Issue 4.

4   Graeme Reid in Sabelo Mlangeni: *Country Girls*, exh. cat., Stevenson Gallery, Cape Town 2010, issuu.com/stevensonctandjhb/docs/sabelo_country_girls_issuu, accessed 26 Oct. 2021.

SA   When did you begin taking photographs?

SM   The first images I took were as a photographer at a wedding. I never actually saw those first images as the bride picked them up directly from the lab. This was in 1997. I now feel as if I have come full circle because I am currently working on a long-term body of work about weddings entitled Isivumelwano. In 2001 I joined the Market Photo Workshop (MPW) and that was an important moment. It felt like a new beginning. I was introduced to photography as a way of speaking about socio-political issues. Photography became a tool to question and engage – it became useful to me in various ways, at a moment when I was questioning power dynamics, the constructs of gender and themes of sexuality. Photography has always been right there.

SA   Did you have any photography influences at this early point in your career?

SM   I began to understand my position as a photographer through the work of Santu Mofokeng, Andrew Tshabangu, David Goldblatt and Ernest Cole. I was also introduced to the big picture of photography and its history as well as a whole generation of masters like Paul Strand, Diane Arbus, August Sander, André Kertész, Bruce Davidson, Robert Frank, Henri Cartier-Bresson and later the Japanese photographers Masahisa Fukase, Hiroshi Hamaya, Tamiko Nishimura and Shomei Tomatsu. But above all, the focus was to go out and make images.

SA   How was your work received among fellow students and teachers at MPW?

SM   I wasn't an 'A' student! To be at school meant that I couldn't provide for my family – which was an issue, as the initial reason I moved to Johannesburg was to find a job. I had to leave MPW classes for months at a time to work. Because of this, I can't really tell you how my work was received. I do remember while working on a class taught by Jo Ractliffe and Terry Kurgan that Andrew Meintjes, a Jo'burg printer, invited me to meet with him after seeing images from my series *Big City*. I guess this was good sign! Later, Jo became my mentor for the Invisible Women series.

SA How do you feel Jo Ractliffe contributed to the *Invisible Women* series?

SM That body of work was part of an official mentorship with MPW. The series documents women who sweep the streets of Johannesburg at night, and initially I was finding it difficult to make a connection with the women. Jo's guidance allowed me to get closer to the subject. Now I am returning to this body of work to reconsider it, and in doing that I am conscious not to erase Jo's voice.

SA You mention that you see these women as 'mothers', but I know you have commented that you view this series as also being about your own mother …

SM I was raised by my mother, and as much as there was a community and extended family who also raised me, my mum was still a single mum. And within our family there were limitations – things that she was allowed to do and things that she was not allowed to do – so her voice was somewhat threatened with erasure. The women I photographed for this series were also threatened with erasure, their labour going unrecognised. I was also thinking about the experience of being a woman in the city of Johannesburg at night and what it means to navigate that space.

SA It strikes me that a sense of place often plays an important role in your photography. You grew up in Driefontein in the Mpumalanga province. Did this location influence your work in any way?

SM Driefontein has its own particular history. It was one of the first areas where Africans could buy land. In the 1980s, under the apartheid government, the inhabitants were threatened with forced removals. However, through community activism, and one particular activist, Saul Mkhize, the forced removals were stopped. In 1983 Mkhize was killed by a white policeman while protesting forced removals. These histories, my relationship to the land, are all important in the work.

SA Apartheid's legacy on land and place also emerges through your other series. For example, in *No Problem* you contrast two communities that exist side by side in Johannesburg – the Alexandra township and the neighbouring wealthy, predominantly white suburb of Sandton.

SM   During the process of shooting in Alex, I felt I was struggling to capture its essence. I wanted to try another approach and for me the contrast between Alex and Sandton was hard to ignore. I decided I would photograph both places and combine them into one series. I also decided to photograph Sandton in colour and Alex in black and white. This change in colour allowed me to speak about closeness and distance between the two places. When photographing in Sandton the security of the gated communities created an issue of access – there were certain places I couldn't photograph.

SA   This contributes a 'surveillance-like' feeling to the Sandton images, a sense of being 'on the outside looking in'. This sense of distance also comes across in the series *My Storie*, a collection of portraits of mostly white residents of Bertrams, a working-class suburb of Johannesburg.

SM   The hurtful and painful thing apartheid took from South Africans is the experience of experiencing each other. Even today, our experience of experiencing each other is still limited because of this history. I photographed in Bertrams over a five-month period but one of the factors that may add to the sense of distance is the fact that I cannot speak Afrikaans. I understand a lot, but I cannot speak it, so there was a communication barrier with some of the people I photographed.

SA   How did you overcome this barrier?

SM   One of the ways I tried to overcome this and get to know the people of Bertrams was to bring notebooks for them to write in. I wanted to find out from them how they felt about the landscape of Johannesburg post-1994.

SA   Through this process you were also invited into some people's houses, for example Martin Botha's. Is there something more to say about this particular image?

SM   Martin Botha was in an accident which left his face disfigured. Martin then experienced complications renewing his forms of identification because of this. He was struggling with this around the same time that I was photographing in Bertrams. For me, this image asks: 'What is identity, and what does it mean to lose it?'.

SA   We've talked about distance in your work but, in fact, a sense of
      closeness and intimacy runs throughout much of your practice. This
      is often born out of a process of embedding yourself in a particular
      community. Can you speak about the process of getting to know the
      people you photograph, of gaining trust and building relationships?

SM   It often begins with looking at myself and the people around me –
      friends, family, church members. These are the people who have
      opened their hearts to me and allowed me to be present in their
      spaces for as long as is needed to complete a body of work. Most
      importantly, it's about sharing the experience of living within a
      community. The camera is secondary, simply a tool to allow me to
      tell stories about the different communities that I am part of.

SA   In some cases, being an 'insider' of the community is particularly
      evident, for example in your series *Umlindelo Wamakholwa*, which
      documents the Zionist Christian Church (ZCC). I believe you have
      been a member of the Church all your life?

SM   Yes, both my parents and members of my family are members
      of the Zion Christian Church. My father is Pastor in a Zion church,
      in fact. When I was seventeen years old, which was the same year
      I was introduced to photography, I left the family church to join
      another Zion church. This was not well received by some of my family
      members. Some of my earliest images document the ZCC, and I
      returned to the series in 2014, at a time when I was concerned with
      the question of being 'born again'. I am a spiritual being, but I have
      had moments, breaks between me and my relationship with the
      church – but I always come back to it.

SA   Could you speak a little bit more about the title of the series,
      which translates as The Night Vigil of the Believers?

SM   Night vigils are moments where the Church comes together, this
      may be for different reasons for example for Osiguqo which is a ritual
      which heals people through spiritual powers. Or it may be a night
      vigil to celebrate two members of the congregation getting married.
      In Zulu, Umlindelo Wamakholwa doesn't directly translate to the
      'Night Vigil of the Believers', because it also means 'the waiting of
      the believers'. So, the translation in Zulu has this double meaning.
      I also wanted to dig into the origins of the word 'believers' too, the
      amakholwa – where the term came from and when it was introduced
      to South Africa. And while we have the amakholwa we also have the

abangakholwa – those who are resisting Christianity. I am thinking about all of these things in the series.

SA   Some of the images in this series seem to have a subtle reference to the roles and perhaps hierarchies between men and women in the church…

SM   In many churches, women are the majority, but they are rarely in positions of power or in charge of decision-making. In the image *Wahamba Umhlaba Sithandaza, Bekabezayo, Nongoma* 2017 you can see male pastors pushing the only female leader among a group of men to the back of the group.

SA   You explore themes related to gender again in your series *Men Only*, could you tell me more about this series.

SM   For *Men Only* I photographed the residents of the George Goch Hostel – a men-only hostel in the East Rand in Johannesburg. I had always wondered what life was like in the George Goch. I made friends with a few residents of the hostel which then led to me staying in the hostel – I was even given a bed. I spent several weeks in the hostel, sharing the daily routines of those who lived there. I was determined not to be swayed by any preconceived ideas I had about the hostel in relation to violence, same-sex relationships or abuse. I found the lives lived there as complex as I had imagined, and at times as familiar as my own skin.

SA   The men in the hostel occupy a precarious position in society, and much of your photography has dealt with those who may be misrepresented, misunderstood or whose stories have remained less visible. But interestingly you have also talked about how 'visibility itself needs to be questioned' – could you say more about this?

SM   A few years ago, I revisited my series *Invisible Women*. I reflected and contemplated on the time I made the work. I started asking myself, 'Why are these women invisible?' This question still haunts me. Over the years as I work, I keep returning to that question – but also to the decisions I took in my work at the time. I have been deeply troubled by that title. What made these women invisible? Why were they invisible? It made sense to me at the time, walking down the clean streets of downtown Jo'burg in the morning, only realising later that the reason the streets were clean was because of these women employed to clean the city at night. My intention with that series was to speak and give a face and dignity to this group of women, and as much as this is clear, the question of the title continues to trouble me. Who is invisible and why? Who declares others invisible and why? What is my positionality as a photographer? What about the agency of the subject?

SA   Do these questions also preoccupy you when considering how you engage with or collaborate with institutions or galleries?

SM   I think the same questions are important when I think about my relations with institutions. The work that I make about different communities sometimes lands in very important institutions and sometimes those institutions themselves are not self-critical, sometimes they render even more violence on marginal communities.

SA   Have you developed a way of working that helps you navigate these issues when choosing how and where your work is seen?

SM   Yes – for example, my photography of the ZCC has been shown in different galleries around the world and the selection of work and title of the show changes depending on the context. In 2017, when it was shown in Museum of Archaeology and Anthropology in Cambridge, UK it was shown under the title *Kholwa: The Longing of Belonging*. I was thinking a lot about the collection of that museum and what other artefacts it held. I wanted to ensure my work wouldn't die like the artefacts that are in this museum. Thinking about the space, its history and the relationship between South Africa and Britain was very important here. When the same series was shown here in Johannesburg, the image selection had a focus on landscapes and considered the church's specific space within the land. It will be exhibited next at an American university under the title *Umvuselelo* which translates as Revival.

SA   This question of context also feels important for your work with queer communities too. For example, *Country Girls* was shot in South Africa, where the country has a constitution that protects against discrimination based on sexual orientation (although hate-crimes and discrimination persist at a high rate). Whereas in Nigeria, where you shot your series *Royal House of Allure* same-sex relations are criminalised.

SM   As you mentioned, the constitution protects against this kind of discrimination in South Africa. This does not mean, however, that

queer bodies are not at risk or that they are always welcome.
In 2021, within two and half months, seven LGBTQIA+ people were
violently killed in this country that supposedly protects LGBTQIA+
rights and bodies. Both South Africa and Nigeria are facing
similar (but not equal) challenges. Here we are protected by law
and yet attitudes can still be hostile and violent. In Nigeria, one
is persecuted by law. In both instances, queer bodies are suffering
and dying.

SA   Yet in *Country Girls* and *Royal House of Allure* you choose to
focus on joy, friendship and love – rather than on homophobia,
hate or pain.

SM   Well, there is this saying – Noma kufiwe kuyahlekwa - which means:
'Even when there is a loss people still smile.' I also work a lot with
suggestion. Sometimes things are not so direct in my photographs,
but they are still there.

SA   It's clear you strike up a very strong bond with the people you
photograph. You even appear in images within series, for example
the playful image from *Royal House of Allure* showing you and Ola.
I imagine it is difficult to part ways with the communities you embed
yourself within.

SM   It is very hard, but I am still in conversation with many of them.
For example, I keep in touch with the people I photographed in
Royal House of Allure through social media. When I finished this
particular project, I did reflect on what it means to make these
meaningful relationships and friendships in a short space of time
and then to have to move on. For sure it's very difficult. For this
project we will be making a book, so I am planning to go back to
visit the community for that.

SA   So, the collaboration will continue. Can I ask how collaborative
your process of photographing is?

SM   Where does collaboration begin and end? For it to be possible
to have the image, the person I am photographing has to be on
board – by allowing me in, but also by creating that space for me.
I can't make my work without the collaboration of the community.
Their willingness to allow their story to be told is an important
part of what I see.

SA   Are those you photograph active players in how the portrait is taken, for example deciding their own pose?

SM   In terms of how the images are made and directing poses, the portraits I made during the Johannesburg Gay Pride parade are the most performative. For these images I would ask people to strike a pose. In this body of work, I feel my experience in fashion photography shows through. It also comes out again in the images from *Royal House of Allure* and *Country Girls* which are more posed.

SA   How important is the idea of taking control of a story to you?

SM   It's very important… not that I am always right. Sometimes I get it wrong, but what I like is that I listen. I take decisions but I listen to input and take that into the process when it is helpful. But when it comes to the story, I don't attempt to take control. The story emerges naturally by itself because the people I photograph are living their lives as they would in any other day. The story will just unfold without my control.

SA   What is the greatest lesson you have learned from the people you have photographed?

SM   The importance of permission and blessings from the persons in the photographs to be part of the collaboration.

SA   Your new series *Isivumelwano* documents wedding ceremonies among Black communities in KwaZulu-Natal, the Alexandra township, and your hometown of Driefontein. What attracted you to the subject of marriage?

SM   The Nguni word isivumelwano represents a contract, agreement or alliance. This series is a celebration and critique of the relationships we keep with others. It is an exploration of the systems we exist in (and against). Traditionally what happens in a lot of South African weddings is that the groom's family will pay lobola – a dowry – to the bride's family, a process which involves discussions and agreements. I think of this in relation to 1994 and the negotiations that took place during that exciting time when the Rainbow Nation was formed. I exhibited the work in 2021 during the unrest across KwaZulu-Natal and Gauteng that followed the imprisonment of the former president Jacob Zuma for contempt of court. This was the worst violence that South Africa had

experienced since the end of apartheid. I remember commenting
at that time that the isivumelwano – the marriage, the contract,
the alliance – was being questioned.

SA   What do you hope to achieve through your photography?

SM   A few fellow photographers and I are beginning to work as a
collective. Working in this way is something that we have been
talking about since 2014. We want to create a space solely
focused on photography, with a strong programme of exhibitions
and residencies. Like the generation before us, which gave
us Market Photo Workshop, our aim is to create a space for
every photographer to participate in our programme through
presentations, symposiums and other activities.

SA   It sounds like you are building another inspiring community,
I look forward to seeing this next chapter unfold. Thanks for your
time, Sabelo.

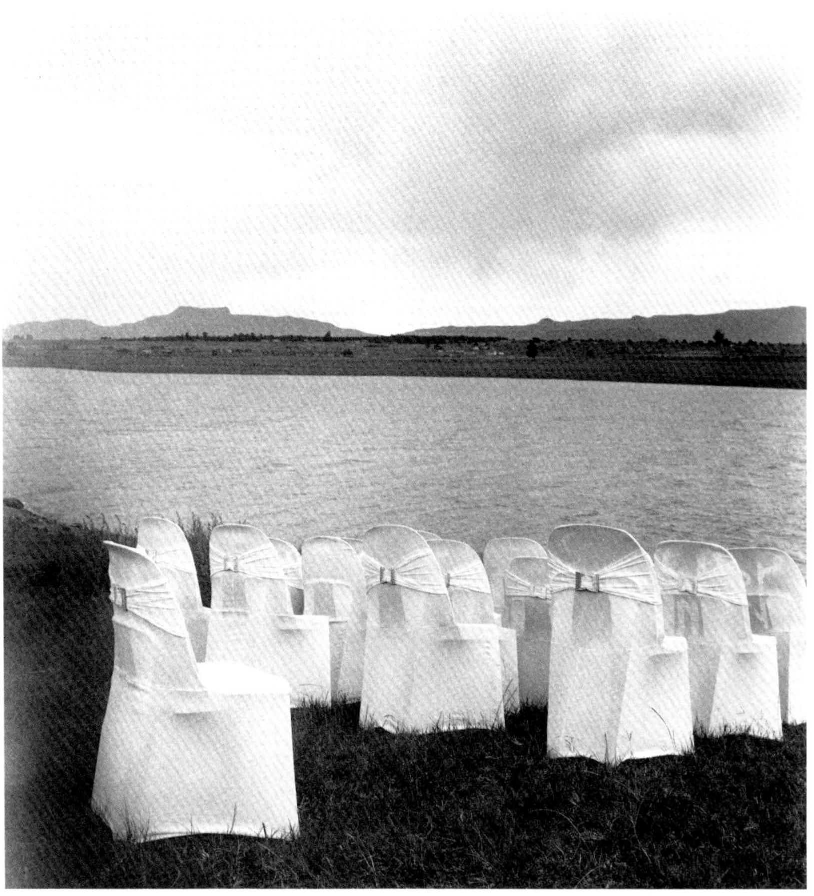

 Ukufika kwengilosi. The coming of an angel 2016 (from the series *Isivumelwano*)

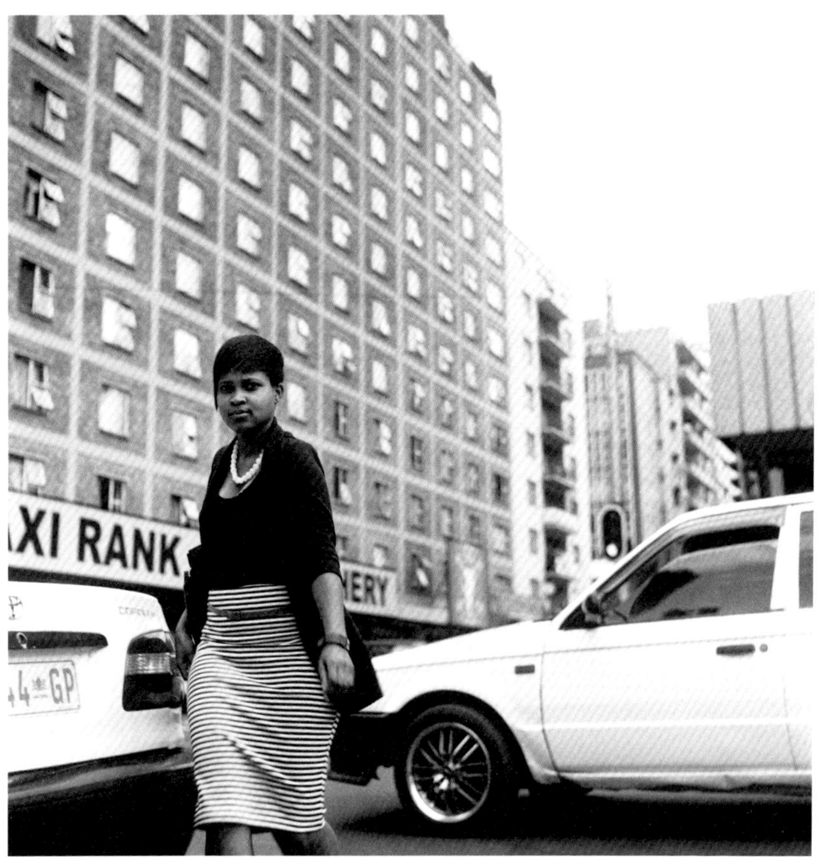

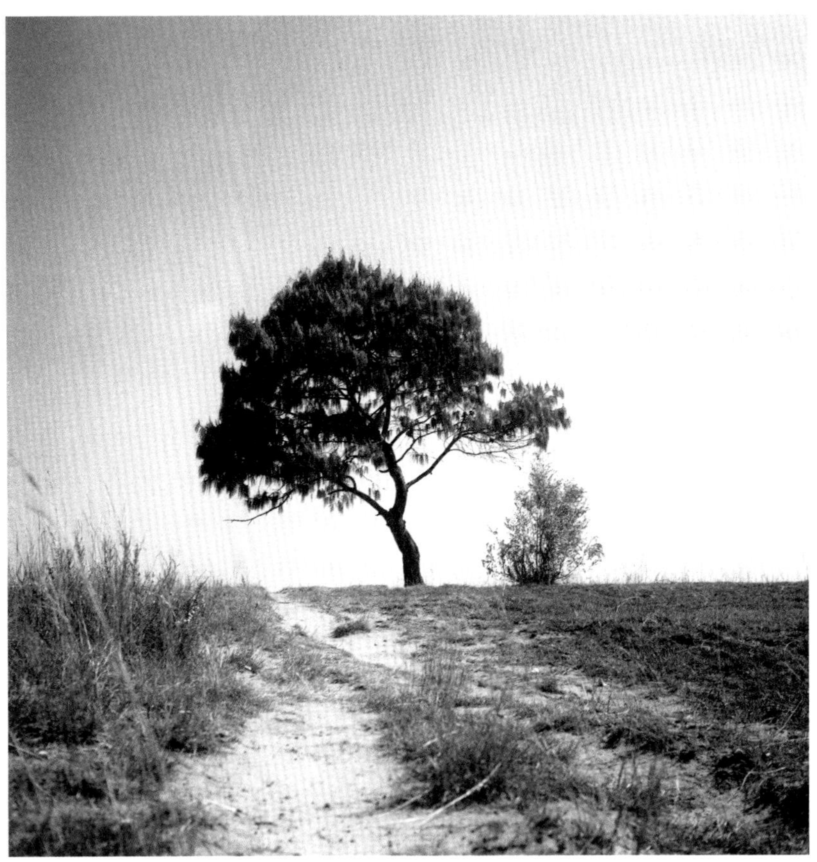

 Home path 2007 (from the series *At Home*)

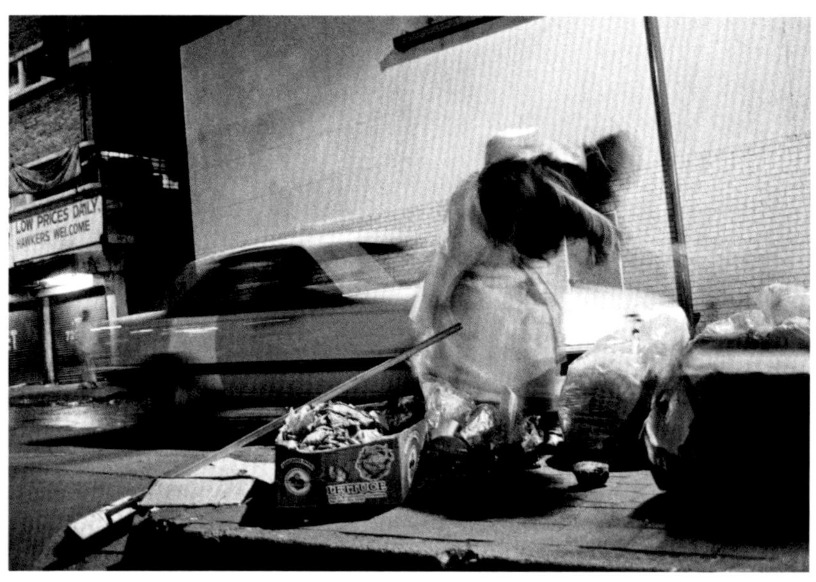

 Umtshanyelo 2006 (from the series *Invisible Women*)

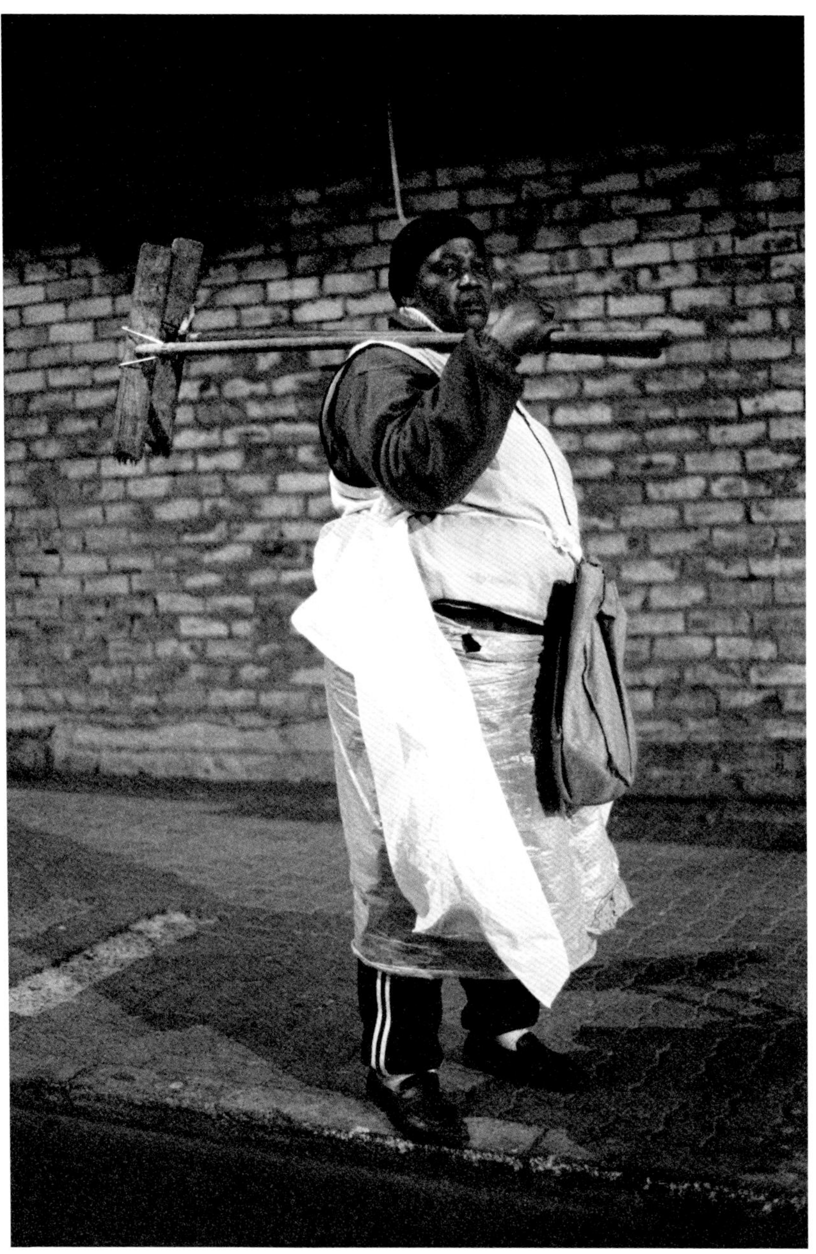

23   *MaNdaba* 2006 (from the series *Invisible Women*)

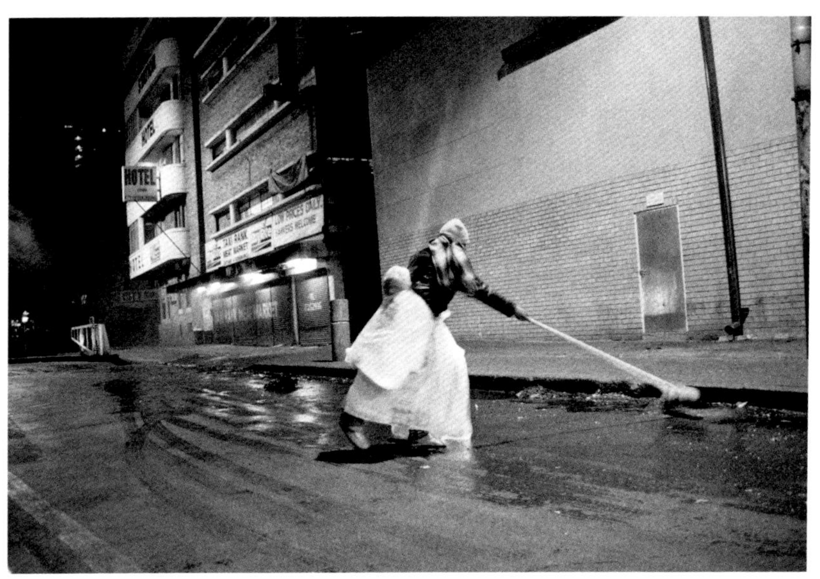

 Low Prices Daily 2006 (from the series *Invisible Women*)

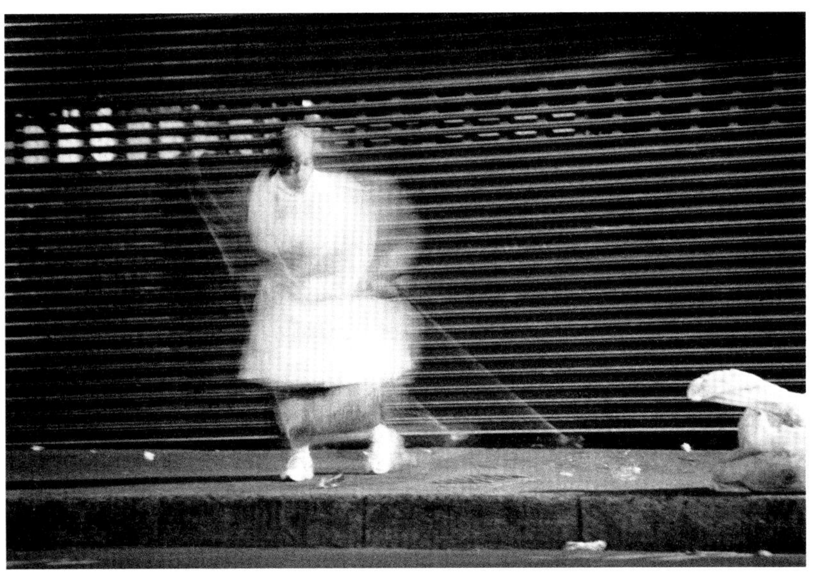

 Invisible Woman ii 2006 (from the series *Invisible Women*)

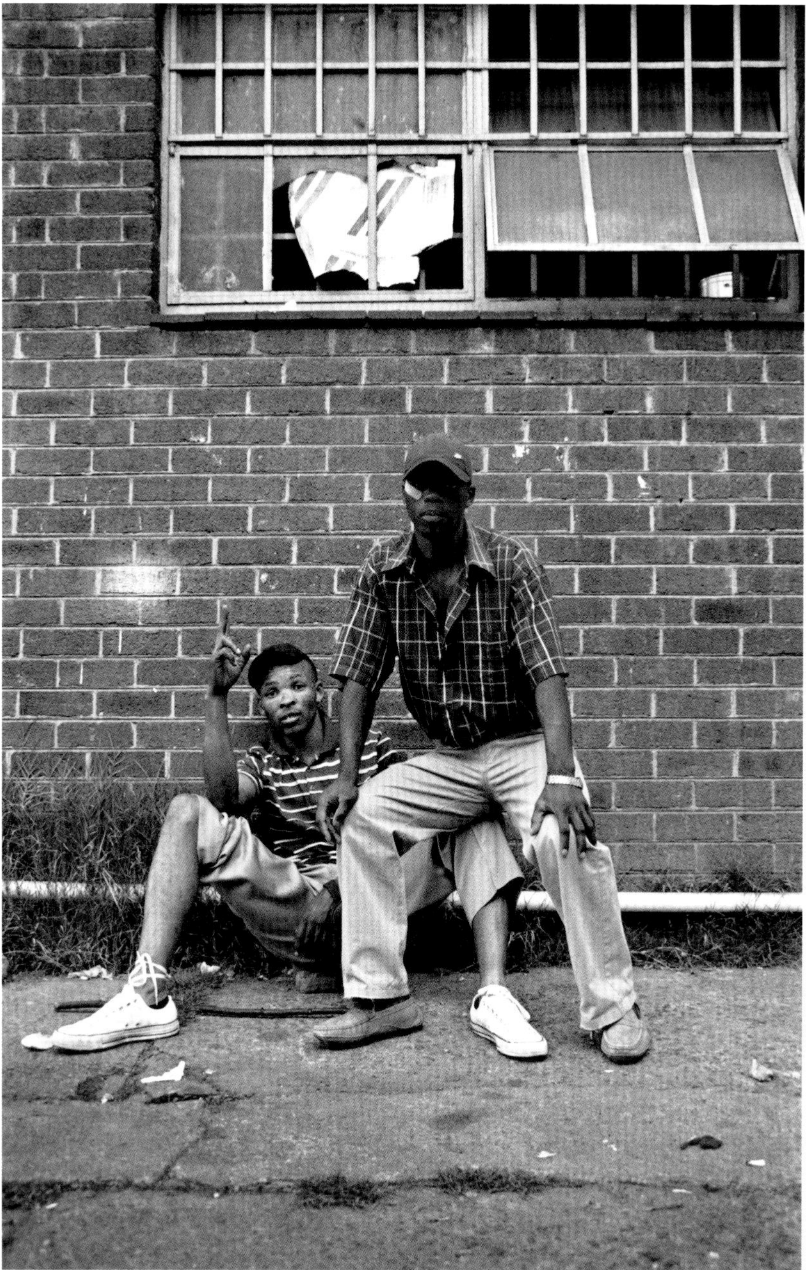

   Room mates 2008 (from the series *Men Only*)

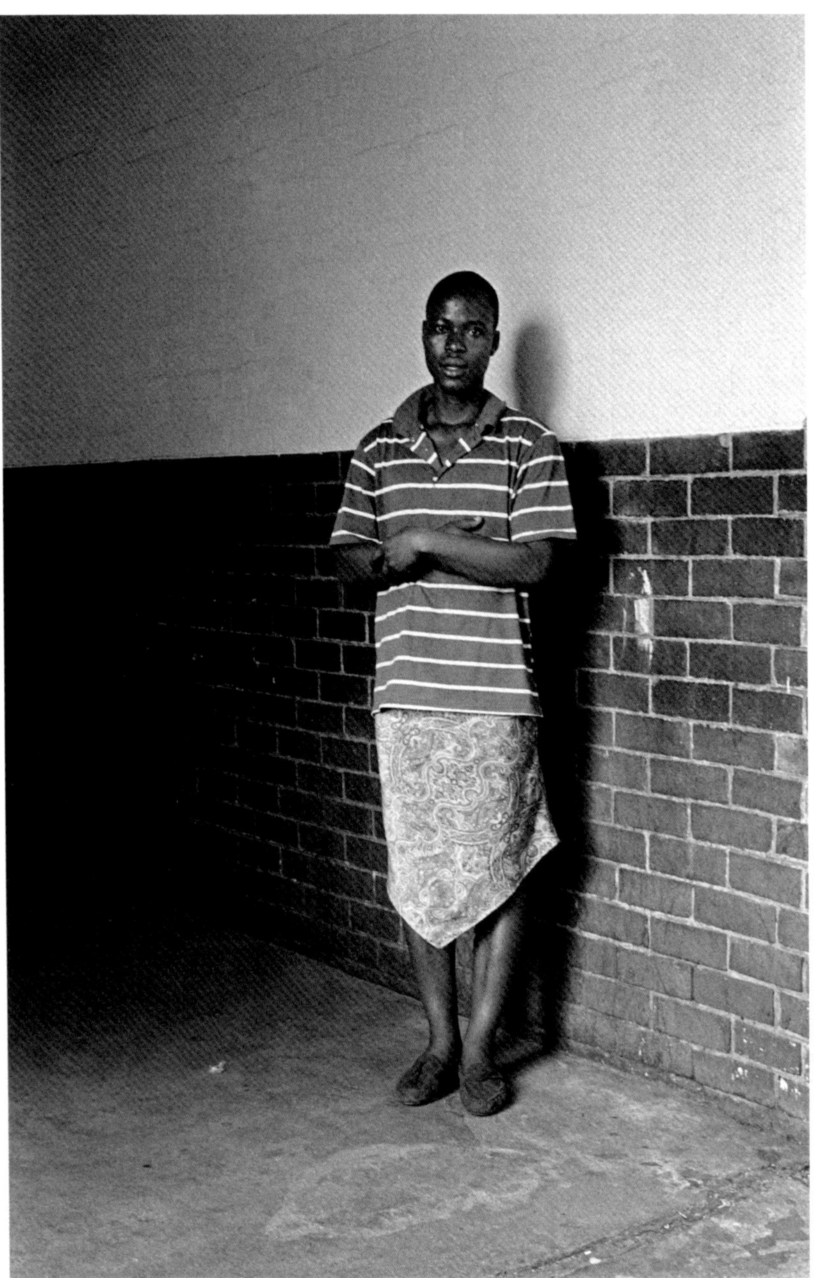

   Mshana 2008 (from the series *Men Only*)

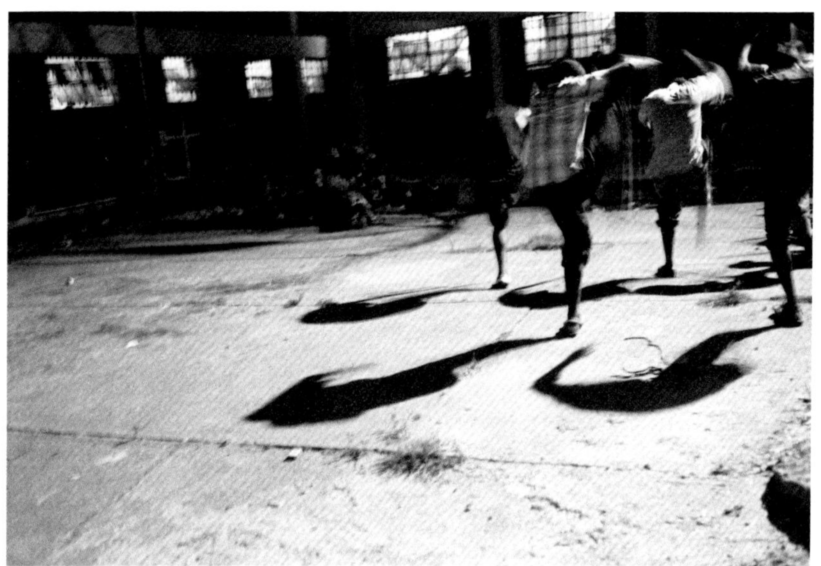

 Practising for indlamu competition 2008 (from the series *Men Only*)

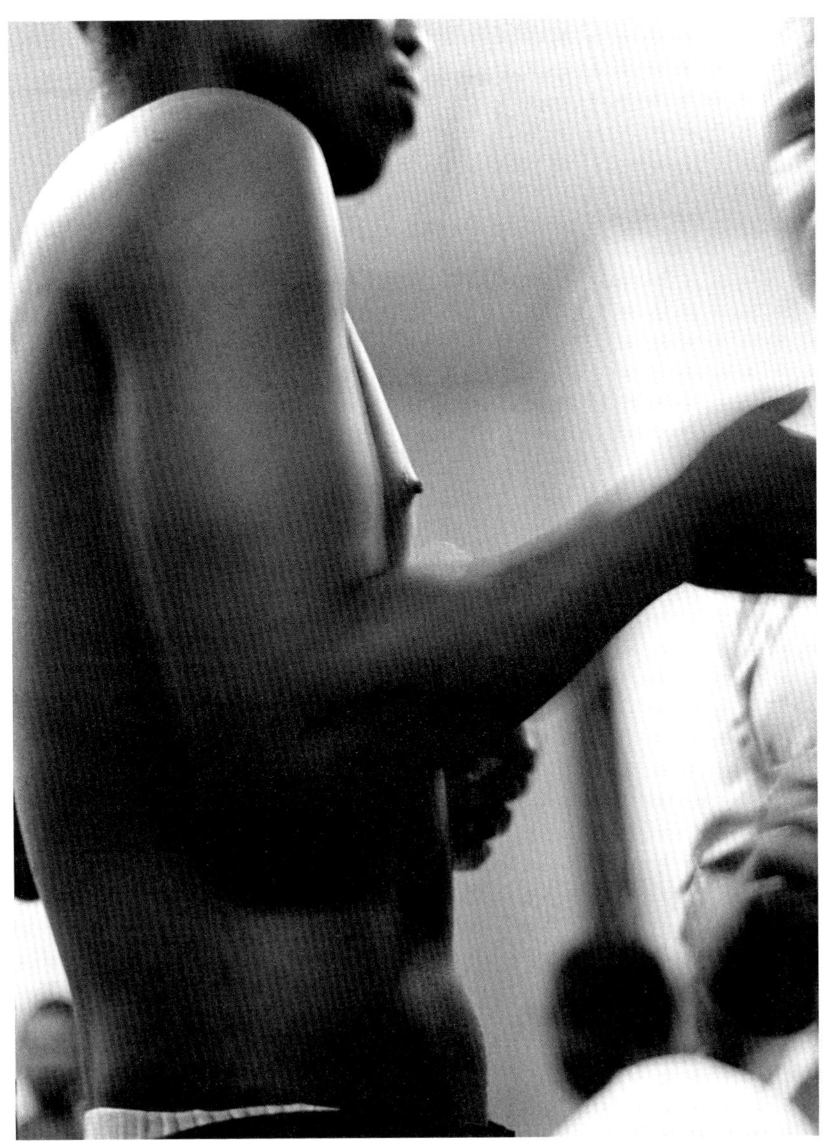

29   *Nipple* 2008 (from the series *Men Only*)

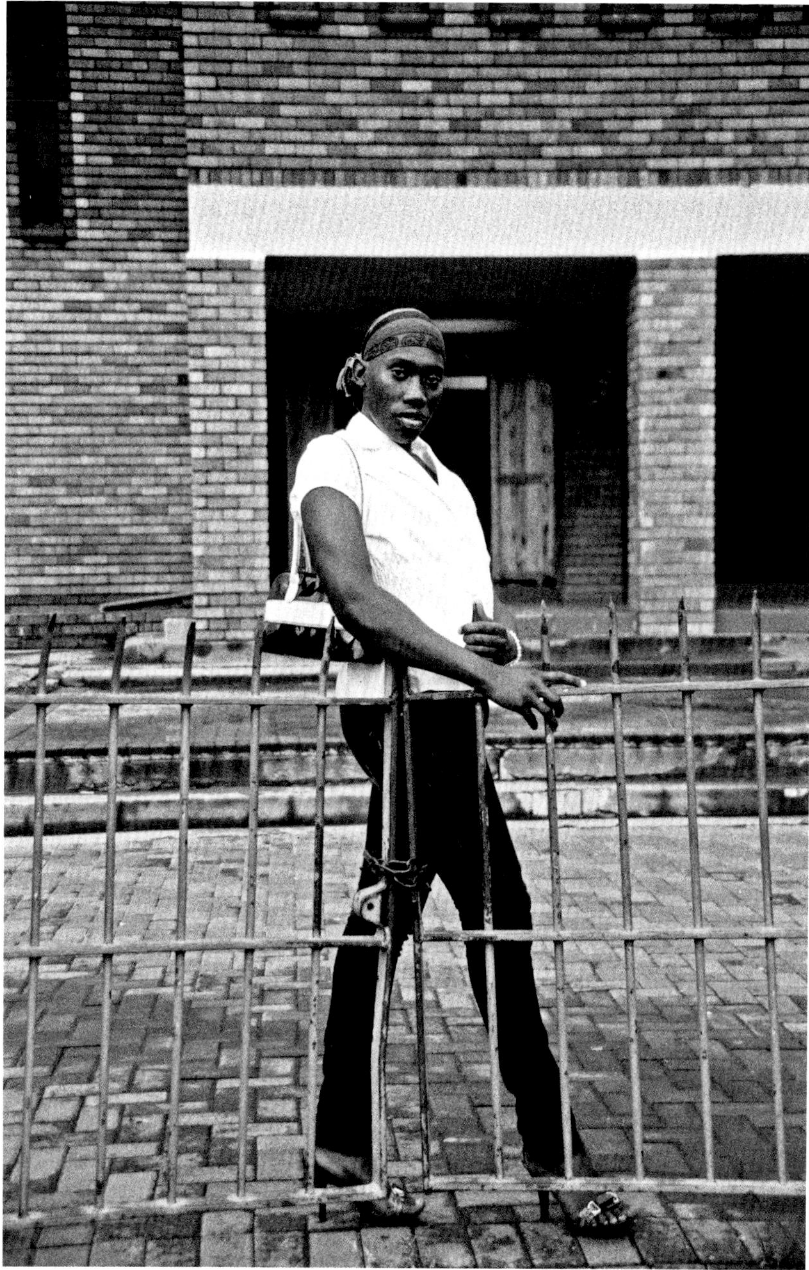

 Xolani Ngayi, eStanela 2009 (from the series *Country Girls*)

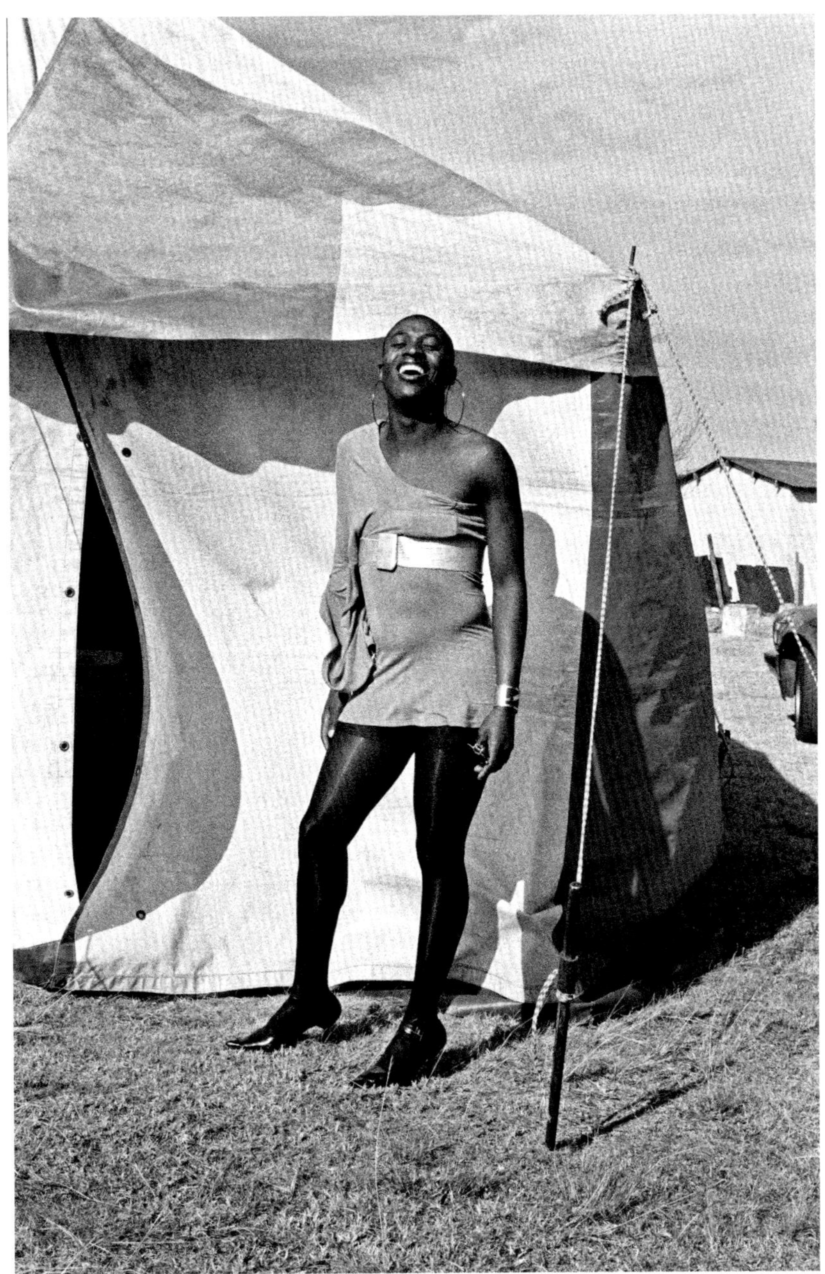

     Bigboy 2009 (from the series *Country Girls*)

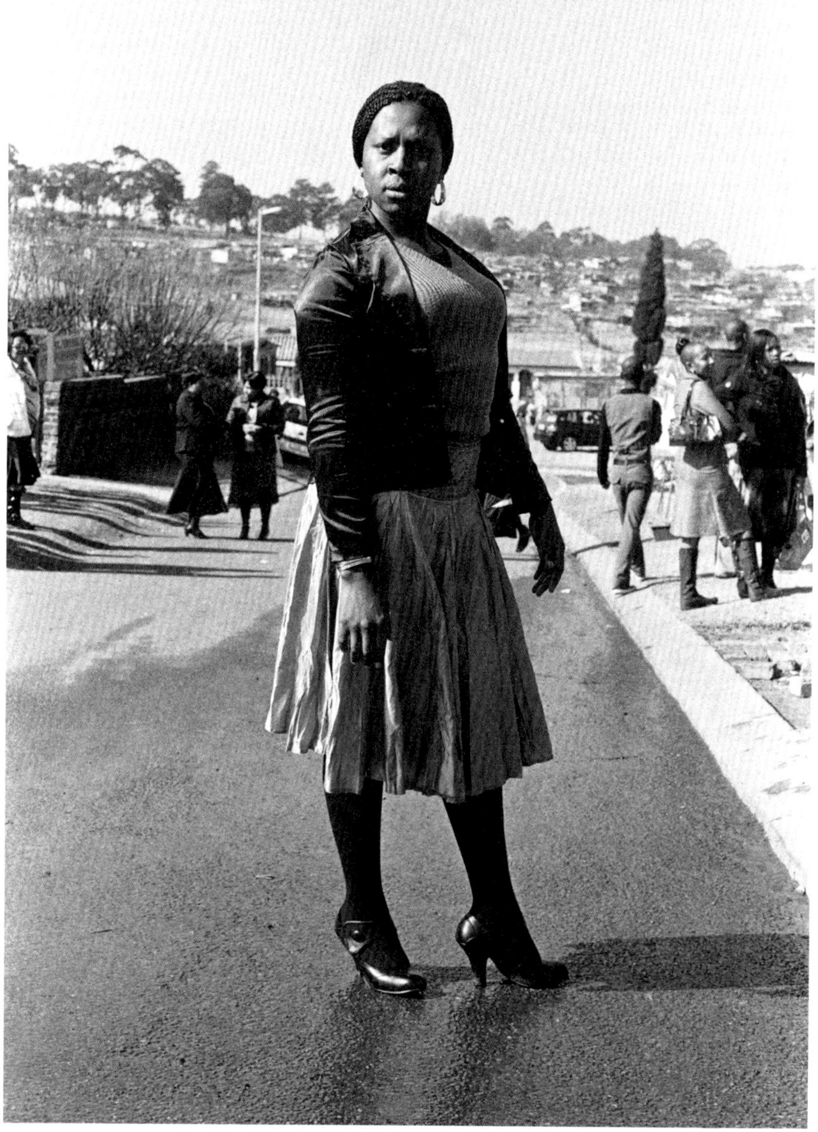

 Madlisa 2009 (from the series *Country Girls*)

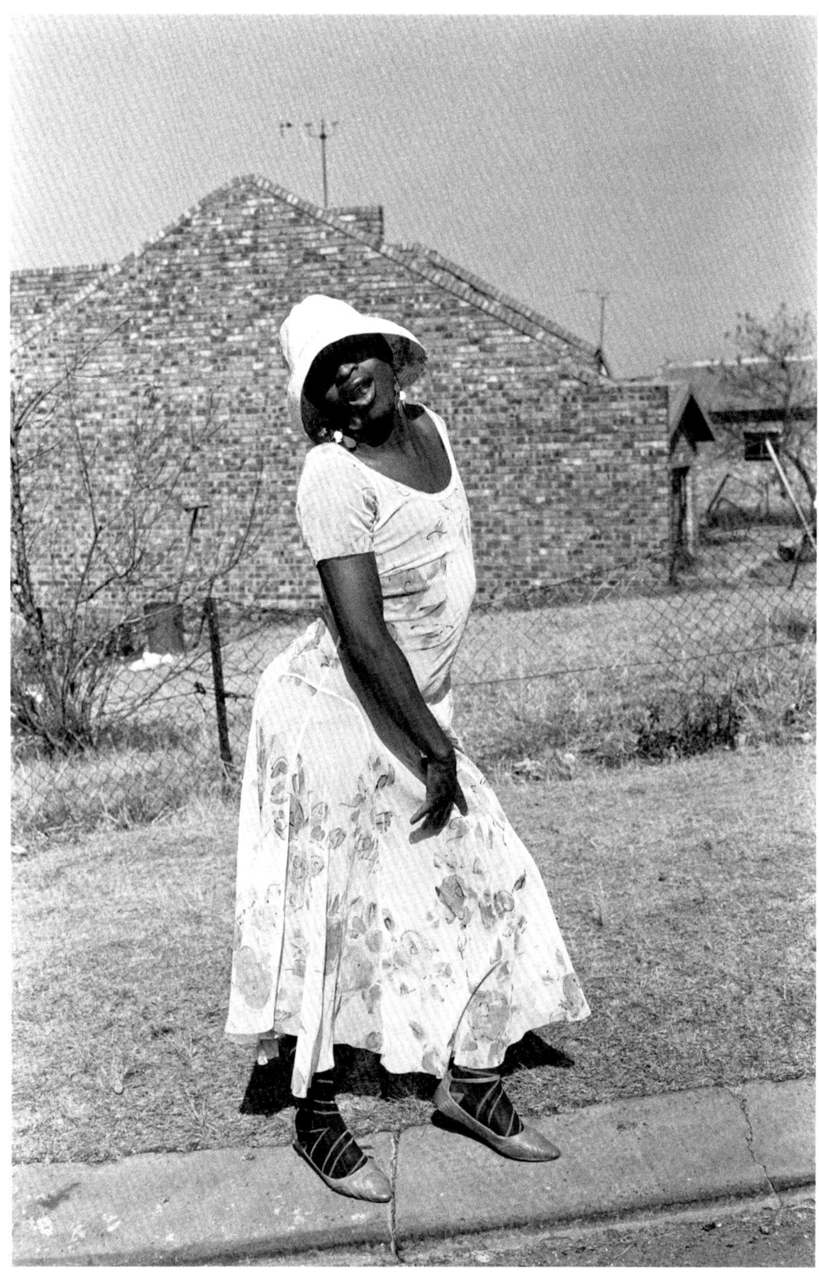

   Lwazi Mtshali, 'Bigboy' 2009 (from the series Country Girls)

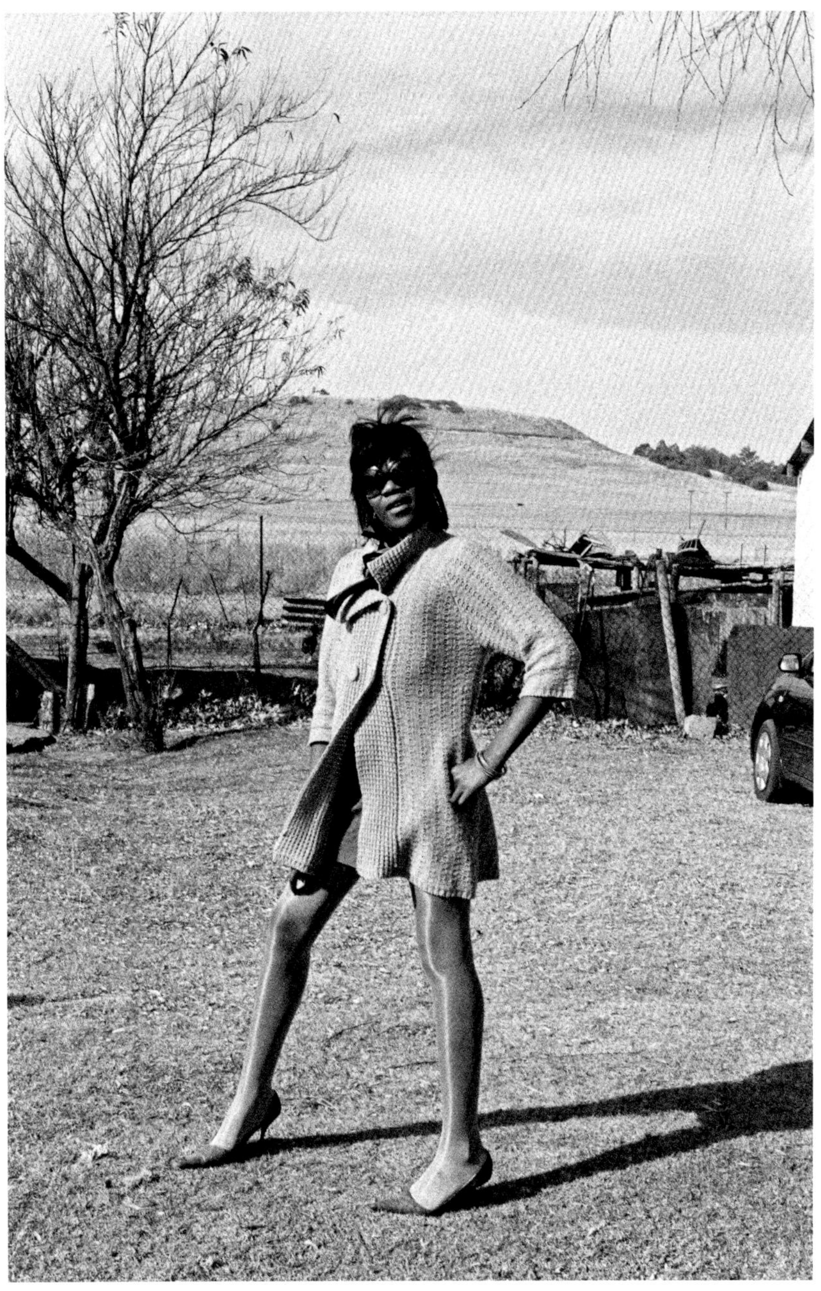

   Palisa 2009 (from the series *Country Girls*)

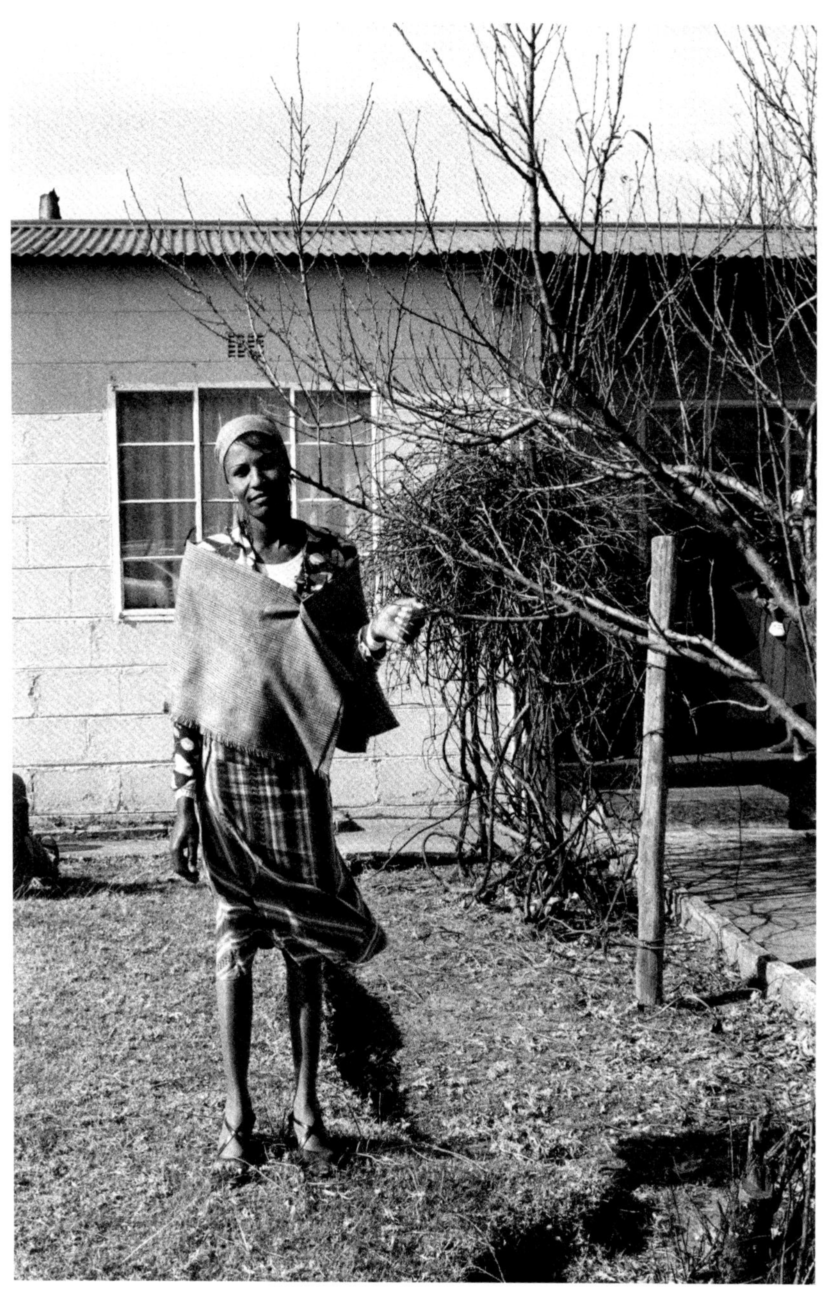

Above: *Innocentia aka Sakhile* 2009 (from the series *Country Girls*)
Overleaf: *Oupa 'Konke enginakho nengiyikho kuyintando KaJehova'* 2009
(from the series *Country Girls*)

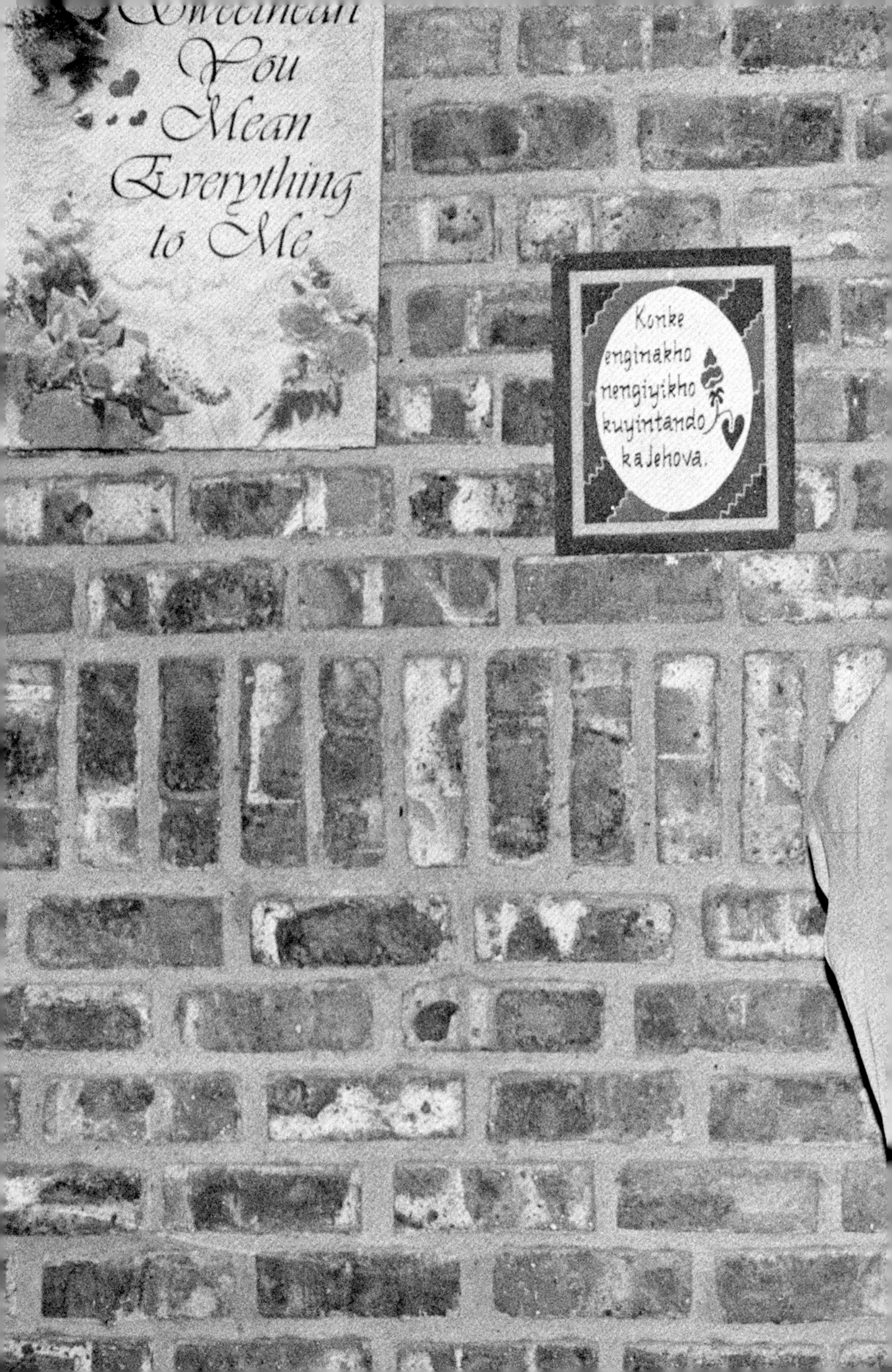
Sweetheart
You
Mean
Everything
to Me
Konke
enginakho
nengiyikho
kuyintando
kaJehova.

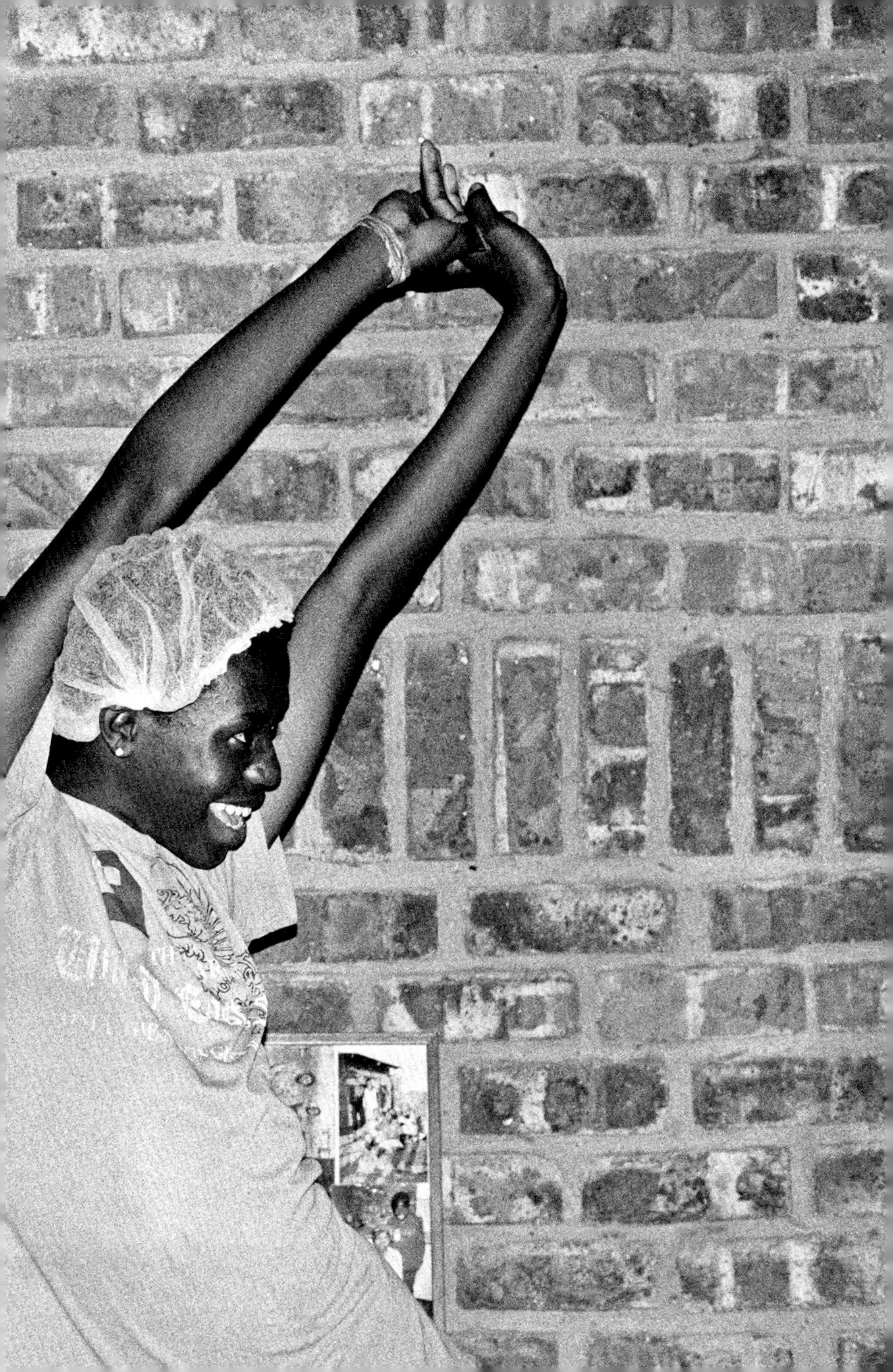

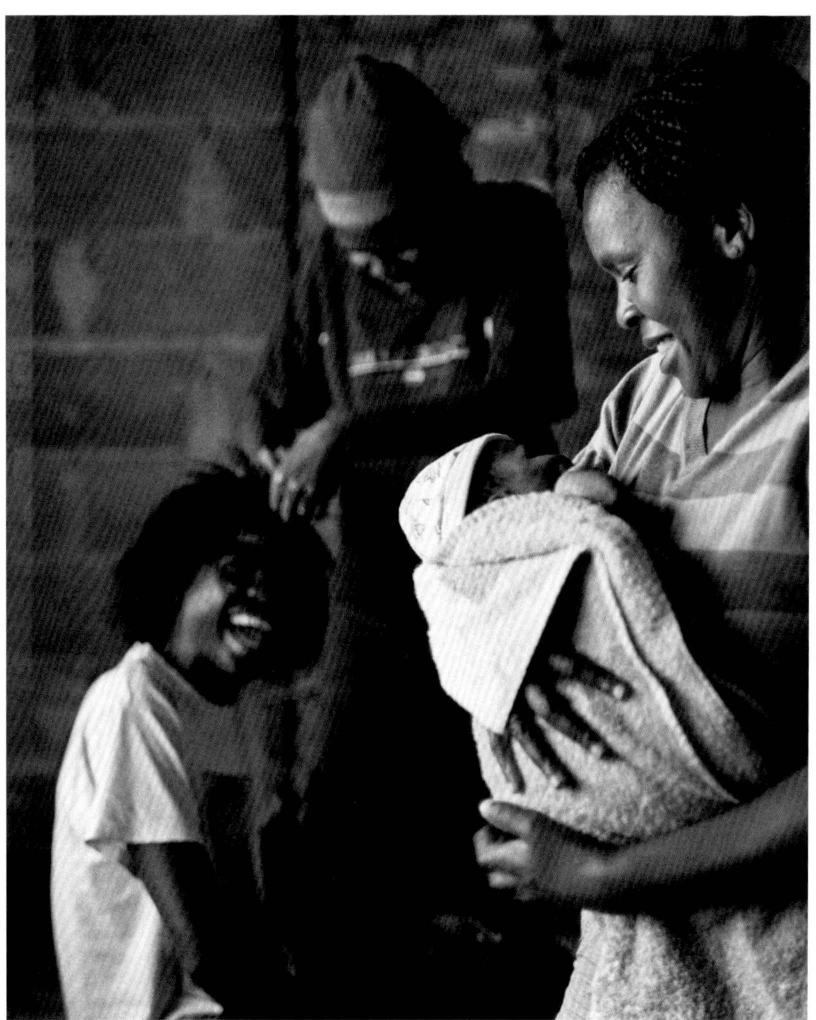

38   *Talent and his girlfriends* 2009 (from the series *Country Girls*)

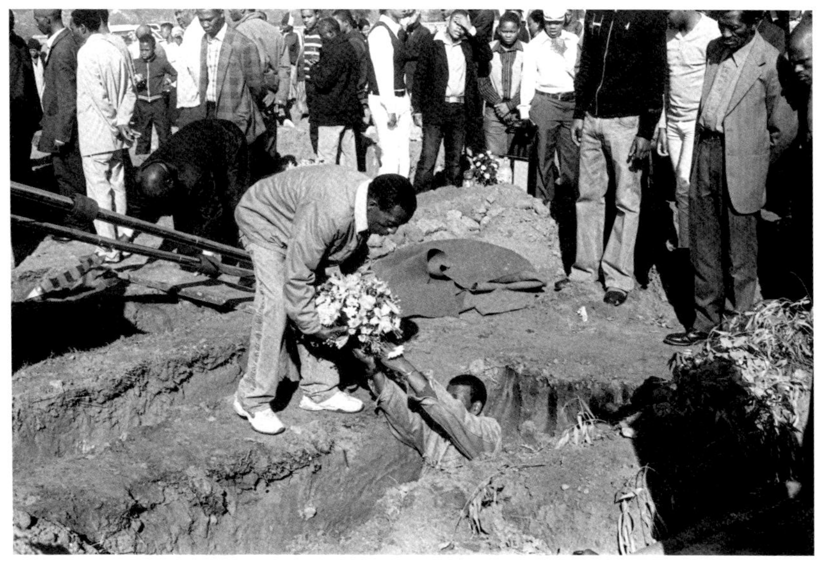

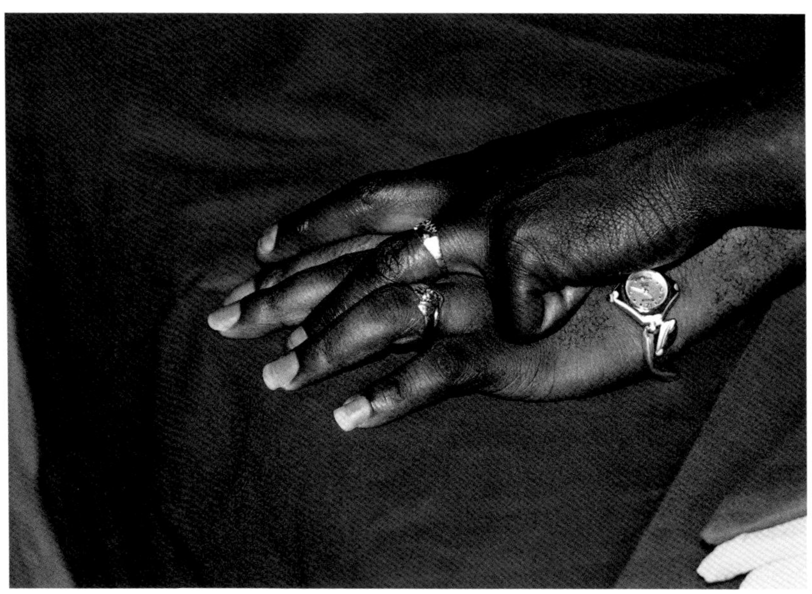

 Top: *Izimbali, Cyprian 'Sonolia' Mbokane's Funeral* 2009; bottom: *Rings, Arthur and Thando* 2003 (from the series *Country Girls*)

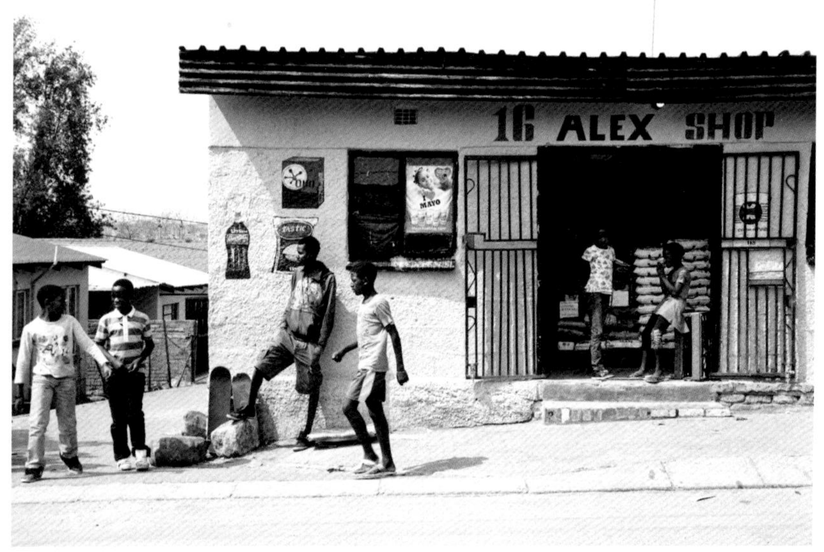

40   *Alex shop, 16th Ave* 2012 (from the series *No Problem*)

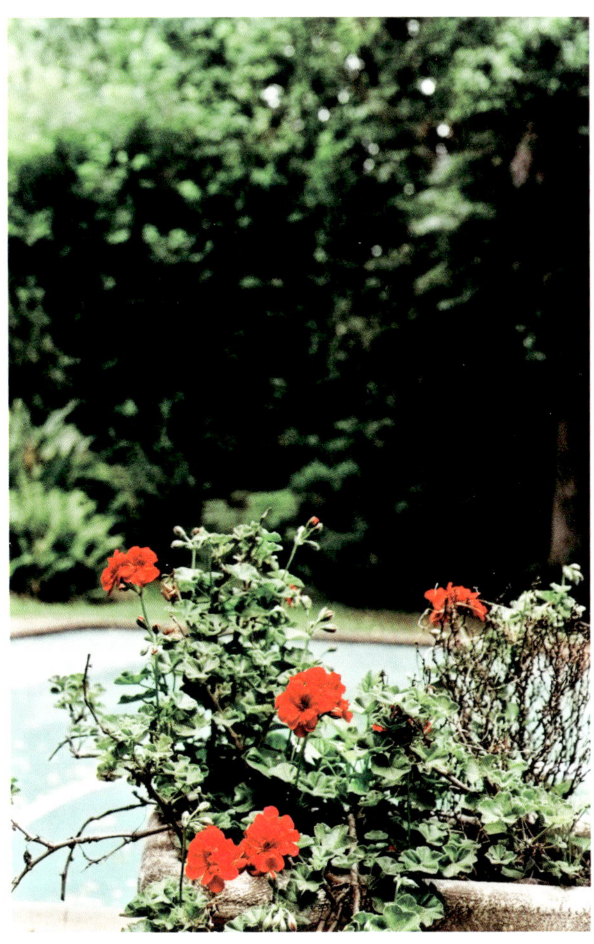

41 *Roses at Hollywood Glen* 2013 (from the series *No Problem*)

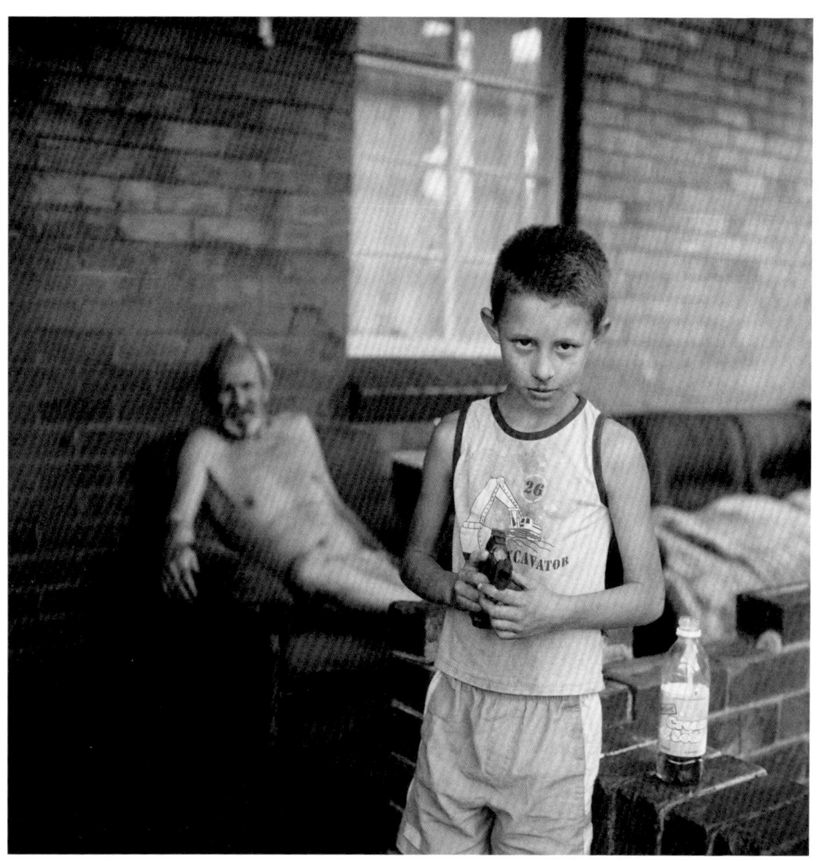

   Shaunny HiFive, 20 Frere Rd 2012 (from the series *No Problem*)

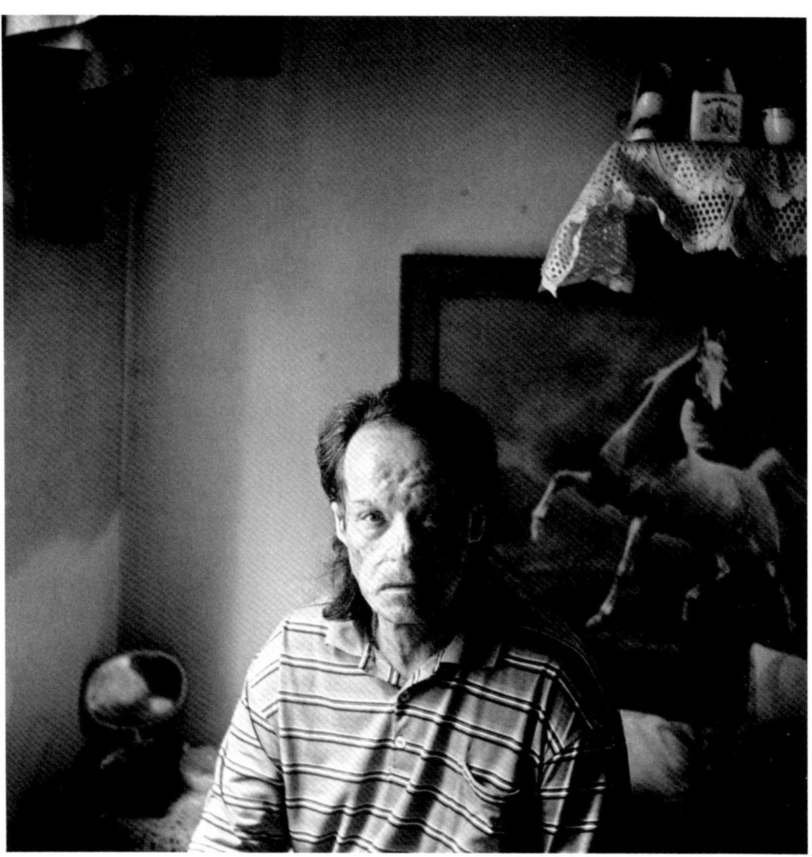

 Martin Botha 2012 (from the series *No Problem*)

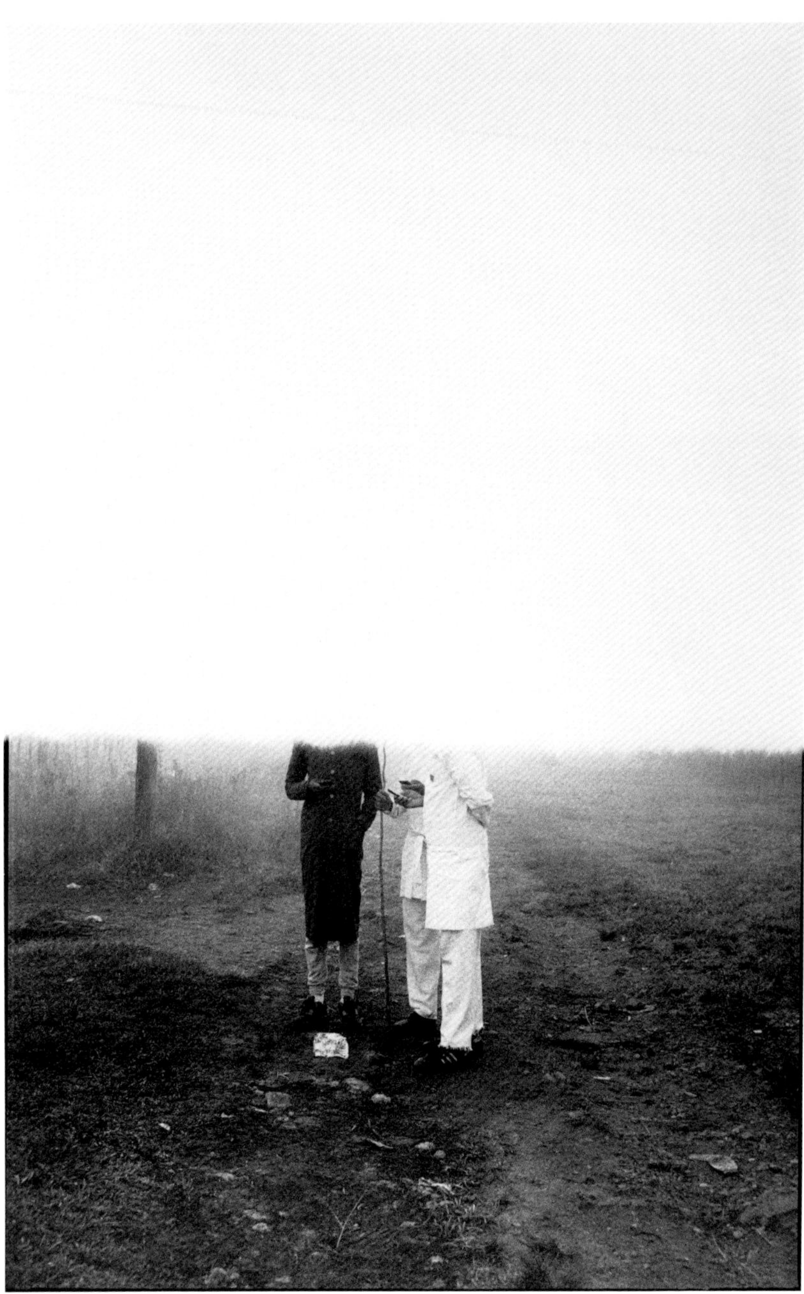

 A morning after Umlindelo 2016 (from the series *Umlindelo wamaKholwa*)

 Umlindelo WaMakholwa 2016 (from the series *Umlindelo wamaKholwa*)

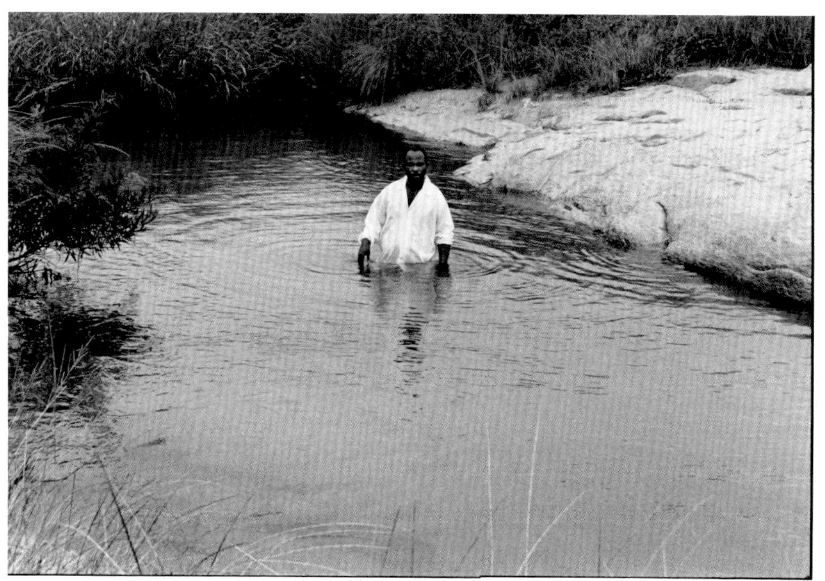

 Mfundisi Ndlangamandla eFernie 2002 (from the series *Umlindelo wamaKholwa*)

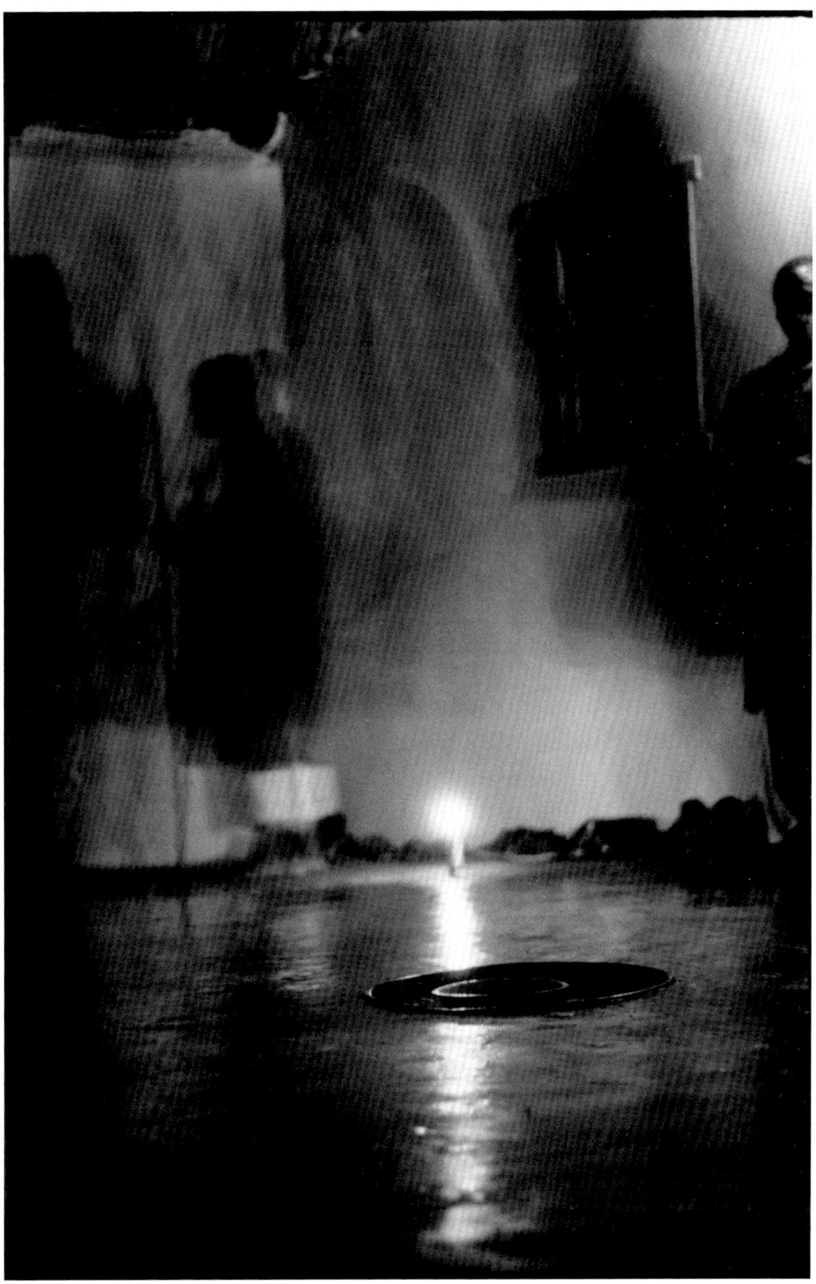

 Imfihlakalo, New Years Eve, Driefontein 2015–16 (from the series *Umlindelo wamakholwa*)

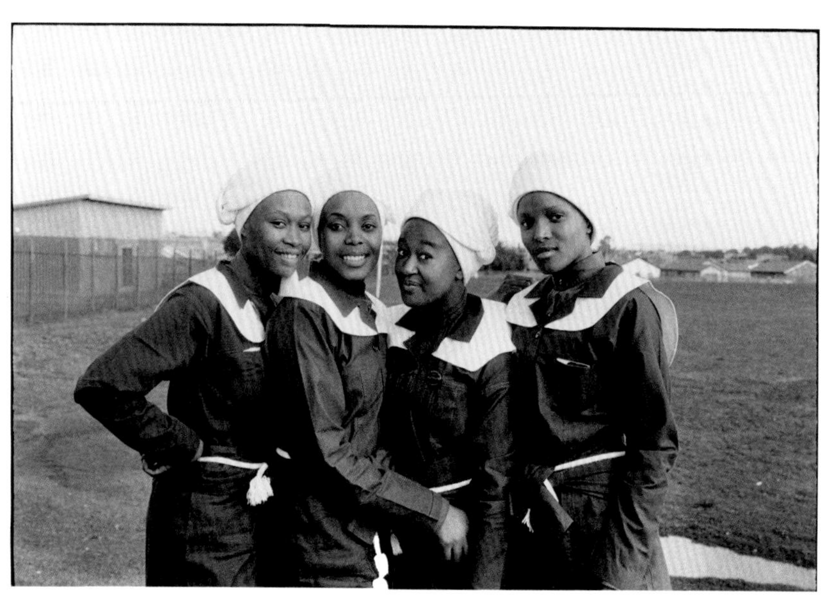

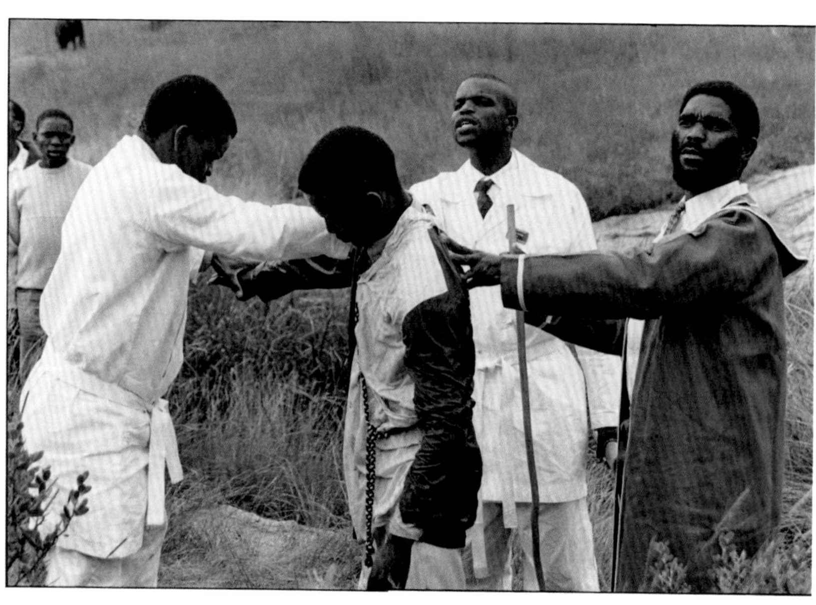

Top: *Ash Maseko, Sarah khoza, Nonkululeko Mbatha, Nompulelo Ndlovu* 2014;
Bottom: *Madoda Thabethe Mabunda Zahkele Mkhize Zakhele Maseko no Mfundisi uNdlela from Swaziland, Esiwasheni* 2003 (from the series *Umlindelo wamakholwa*)

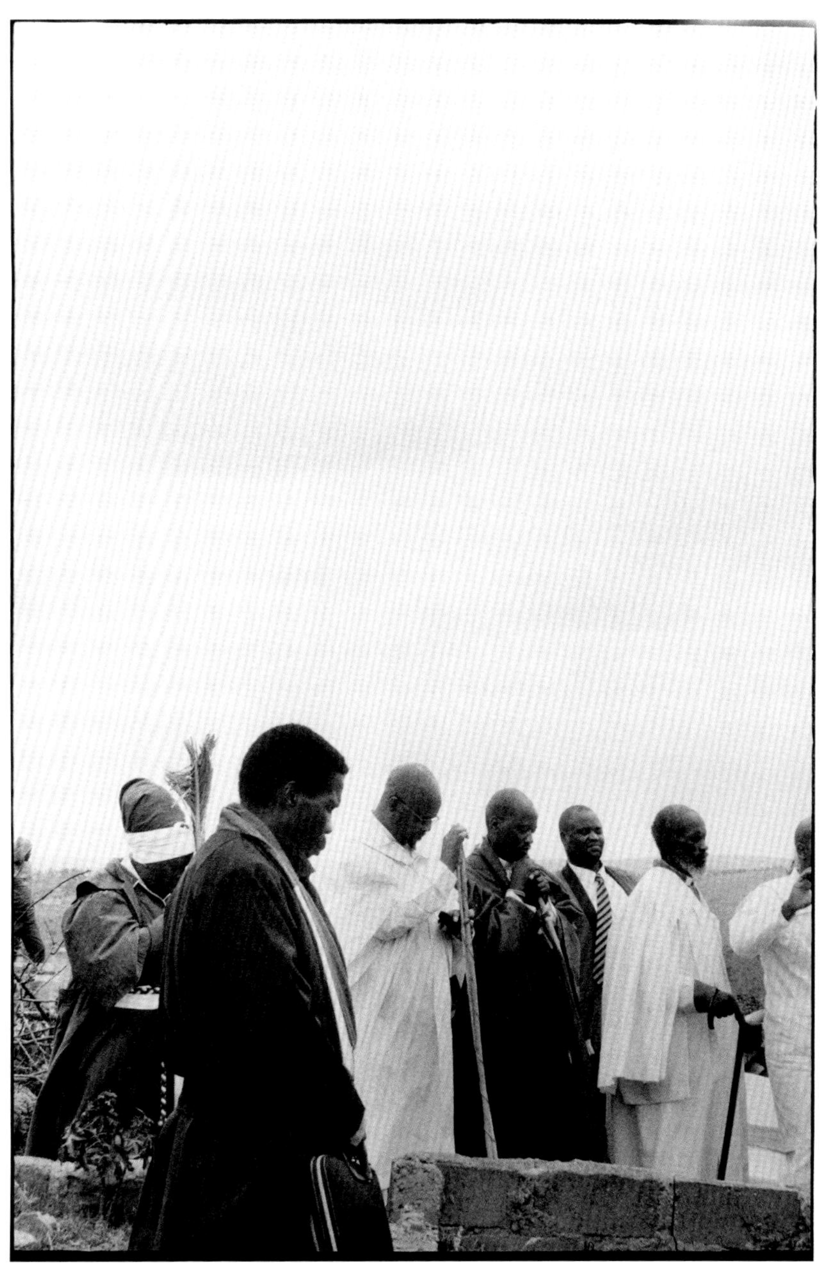

Wahamba uhlaba sithandaza, Bhekabezayo, Nongoma 2017 (from the series
Unlindelo wamakholwa)

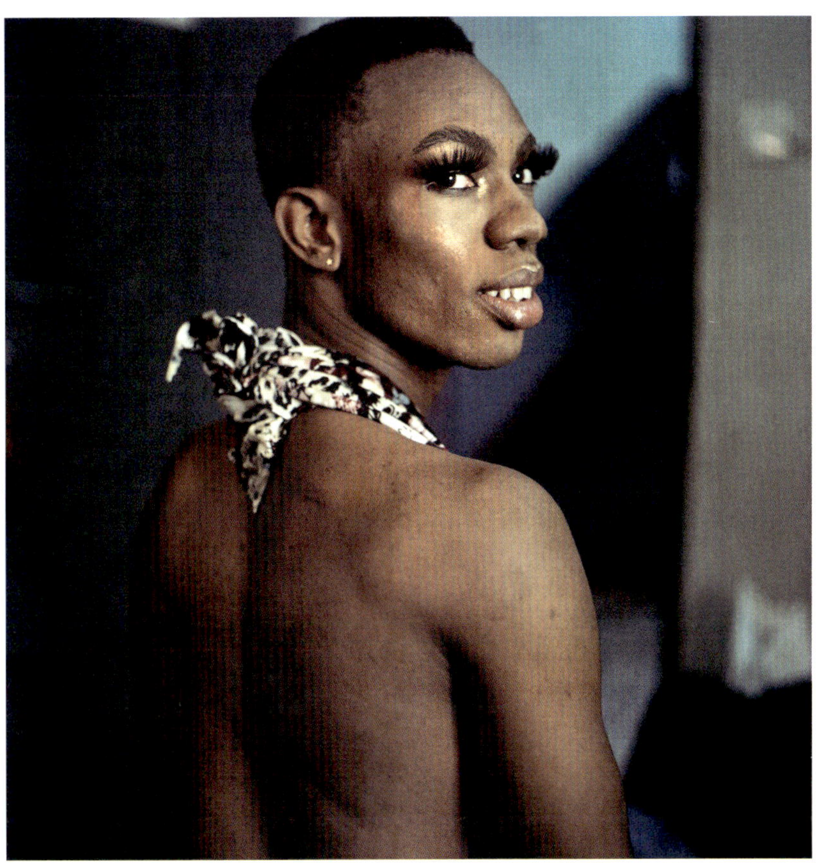

  James Brown 2019 (from the series *The Royal House of Allure*)

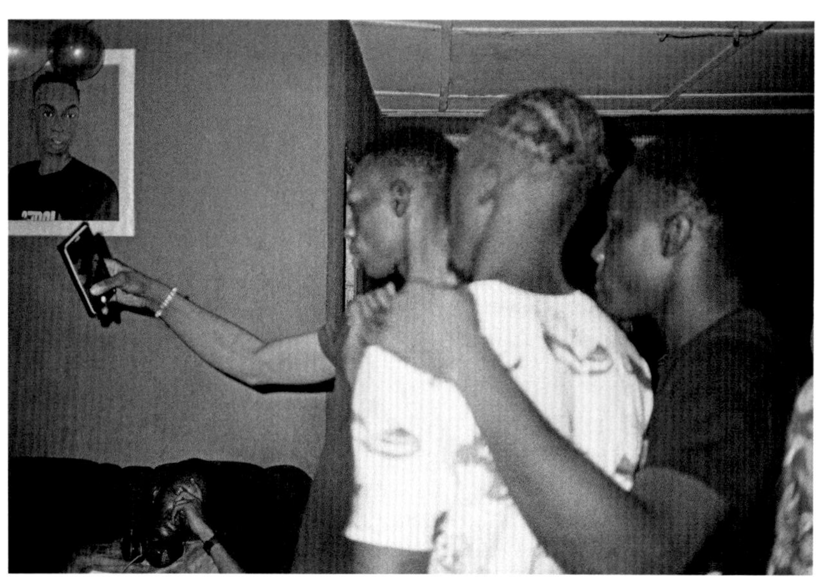

A selfie with social media influencer James Brown at a party 2019
(from the series *The Royal House of Allure*)

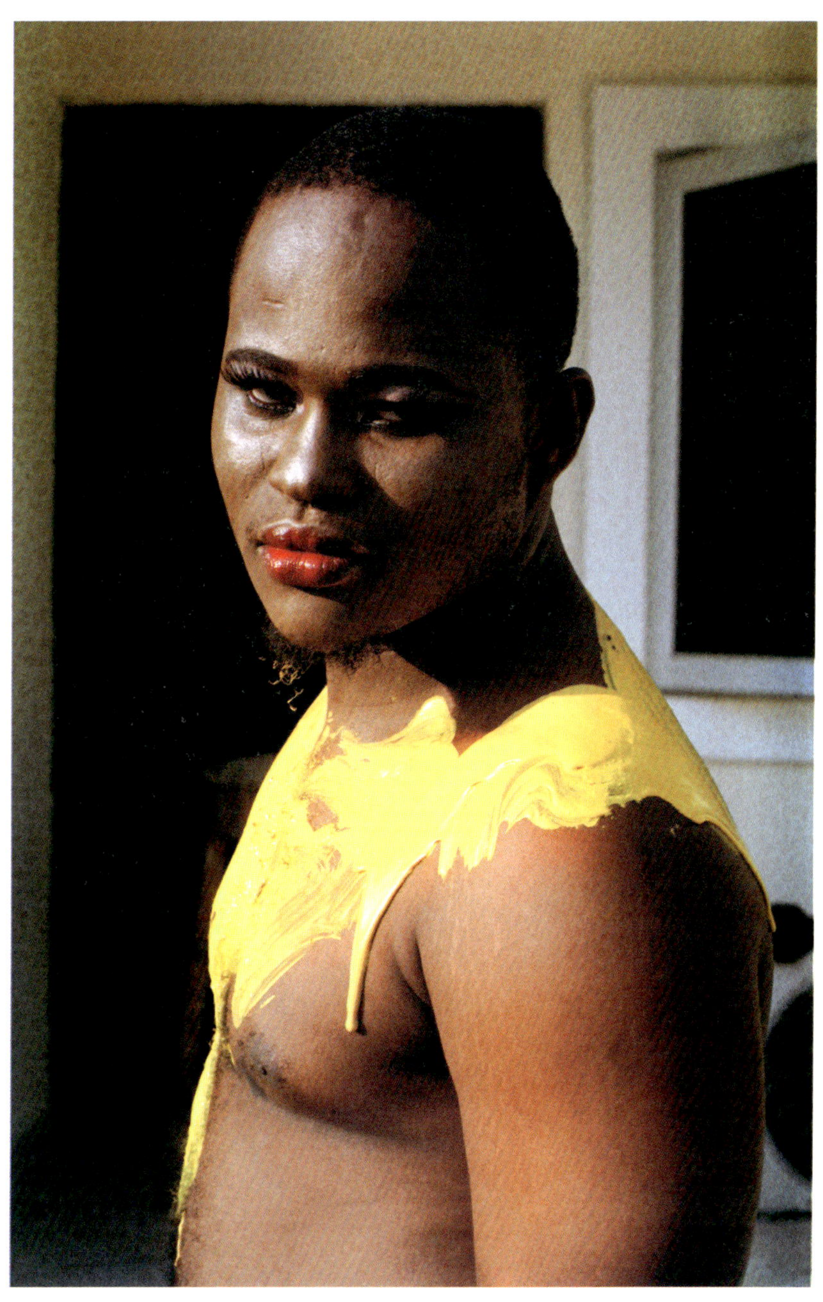

Olalere's body painting shoot (make up artist Thom Smith and Daniel) 2019
(from the series *The Royal House of Allure*)

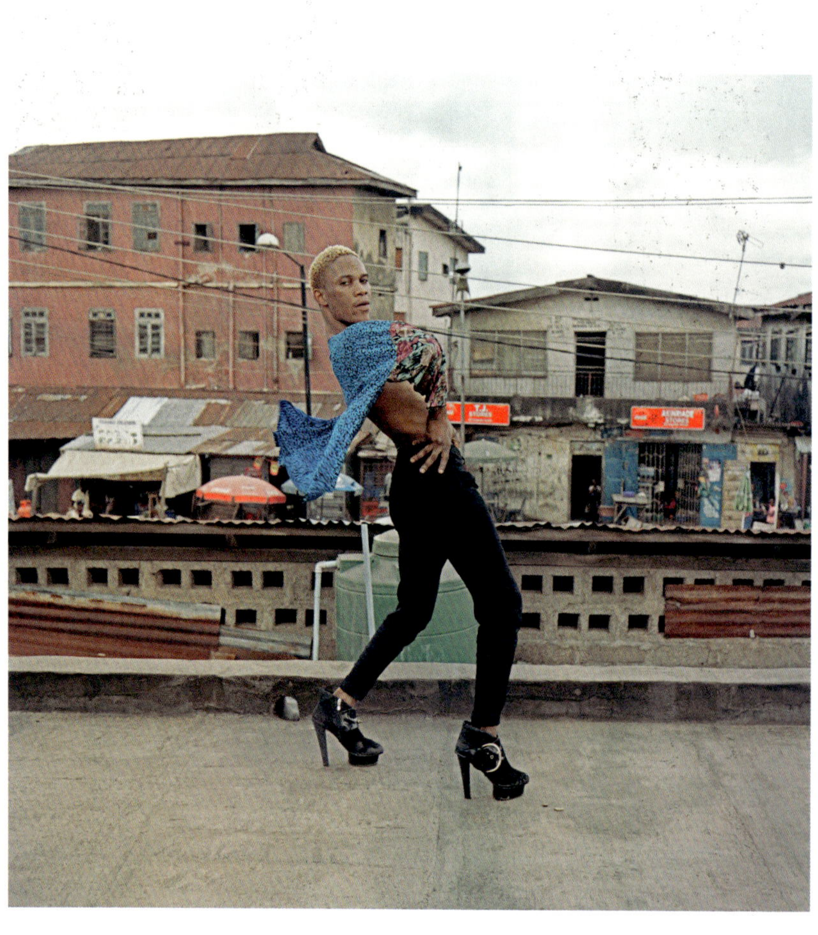

A roof top photoshoot with the dancers; Tonnex, (Ruby, Nonso and Oshodi) 2019
(from the series *The Royal House of Allure*)

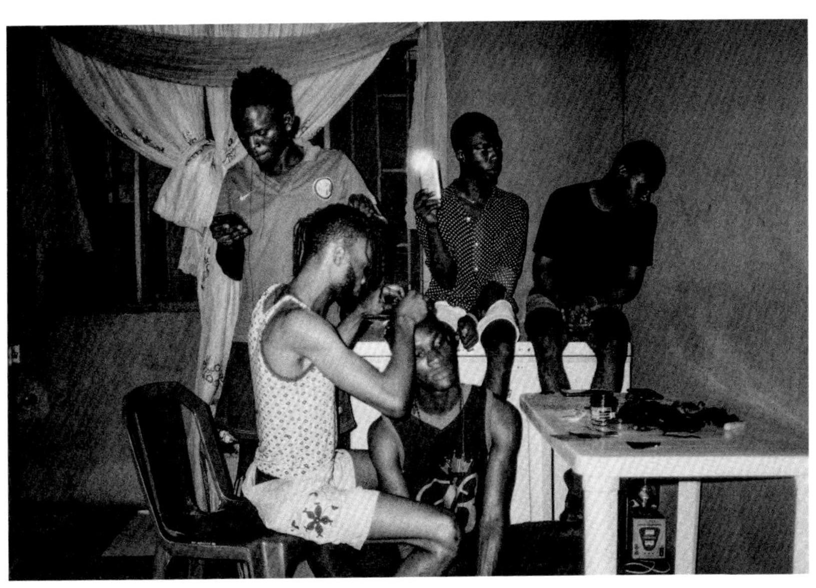

No Nepa evening with Nonso, Thom, Mike, Daniel and Ruby 2019
(from the series *The Royal House of Allure*)

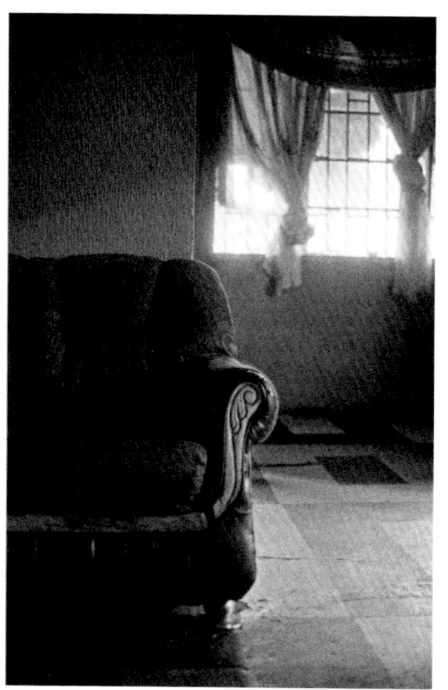

  The couch (never empty) 2019 (from the series *The Royal House of Allure*)

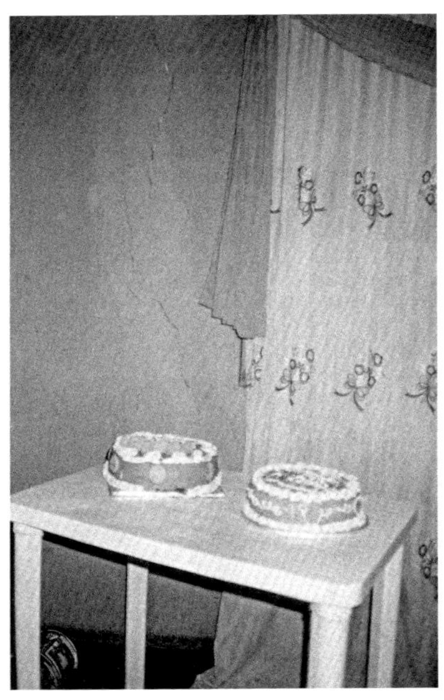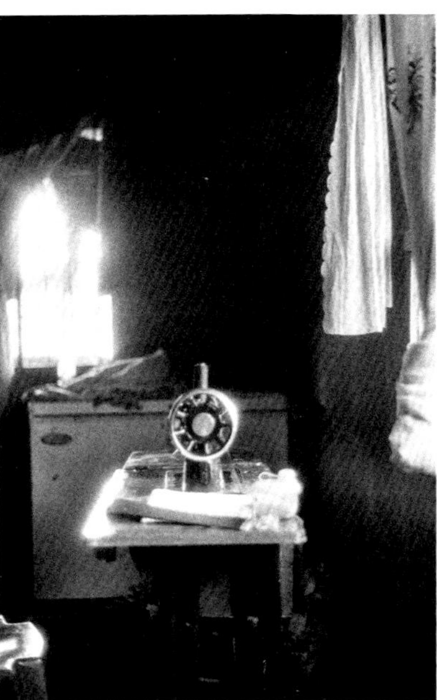

 Birthday cake 2019 (from the series *The Royal House of Allure*)

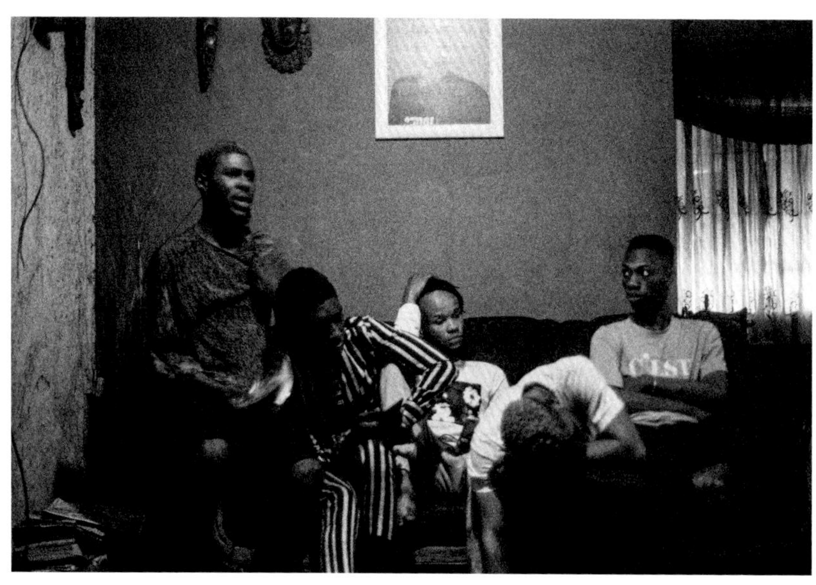

*Sharing family experiences. Ruby, Daniel, Thom Smith, Tonnex and James
Brown (Mr Morrison, Jayder, Lil B, Nandi, Ola, Mohammed) 2019 (from the series
The Royal House of Allure)*

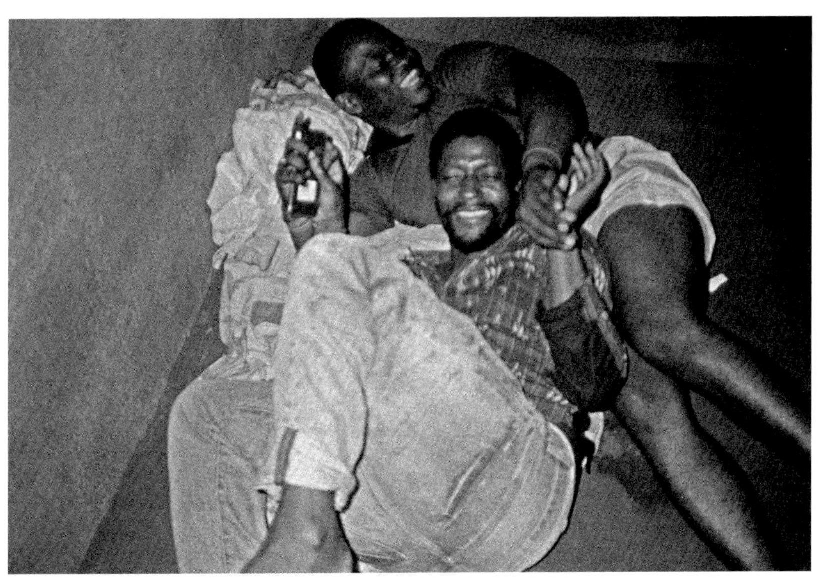

Afternoon visit, Ola and I playing nipple, photo by Sodiq 2019
(from the series *The Royal House of Allure*)

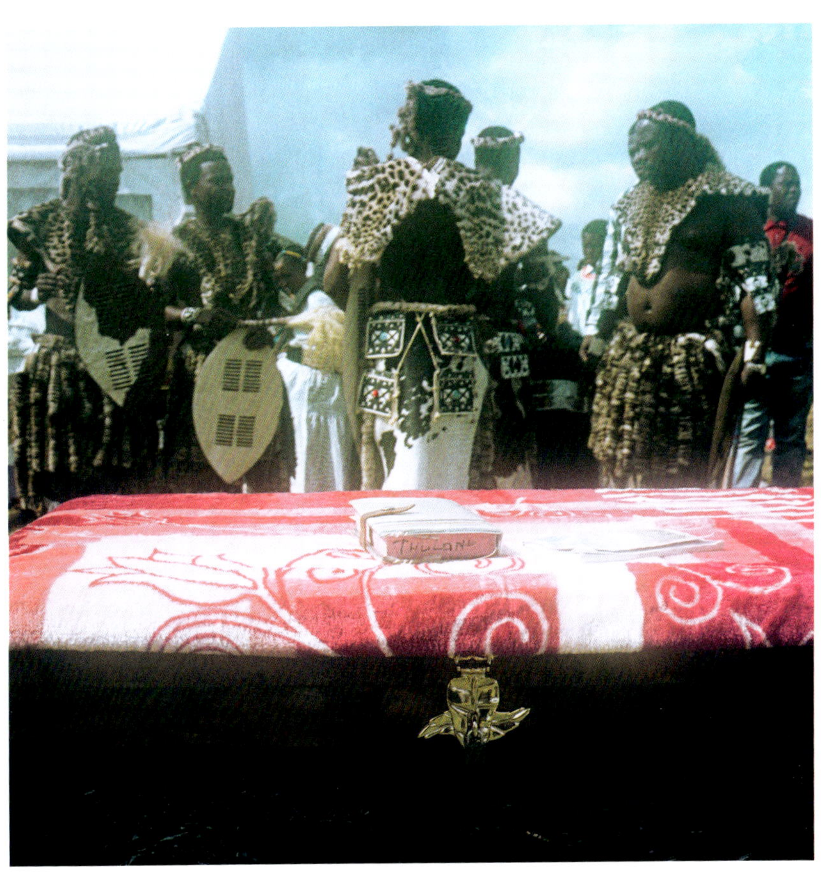

Above: *Thulani. Ibhayibheli before us* 2017 (from the series *Isivumelwano*)
Overleaf: *Beautiful Love* 2003 (from the series *Isivumelwano*)

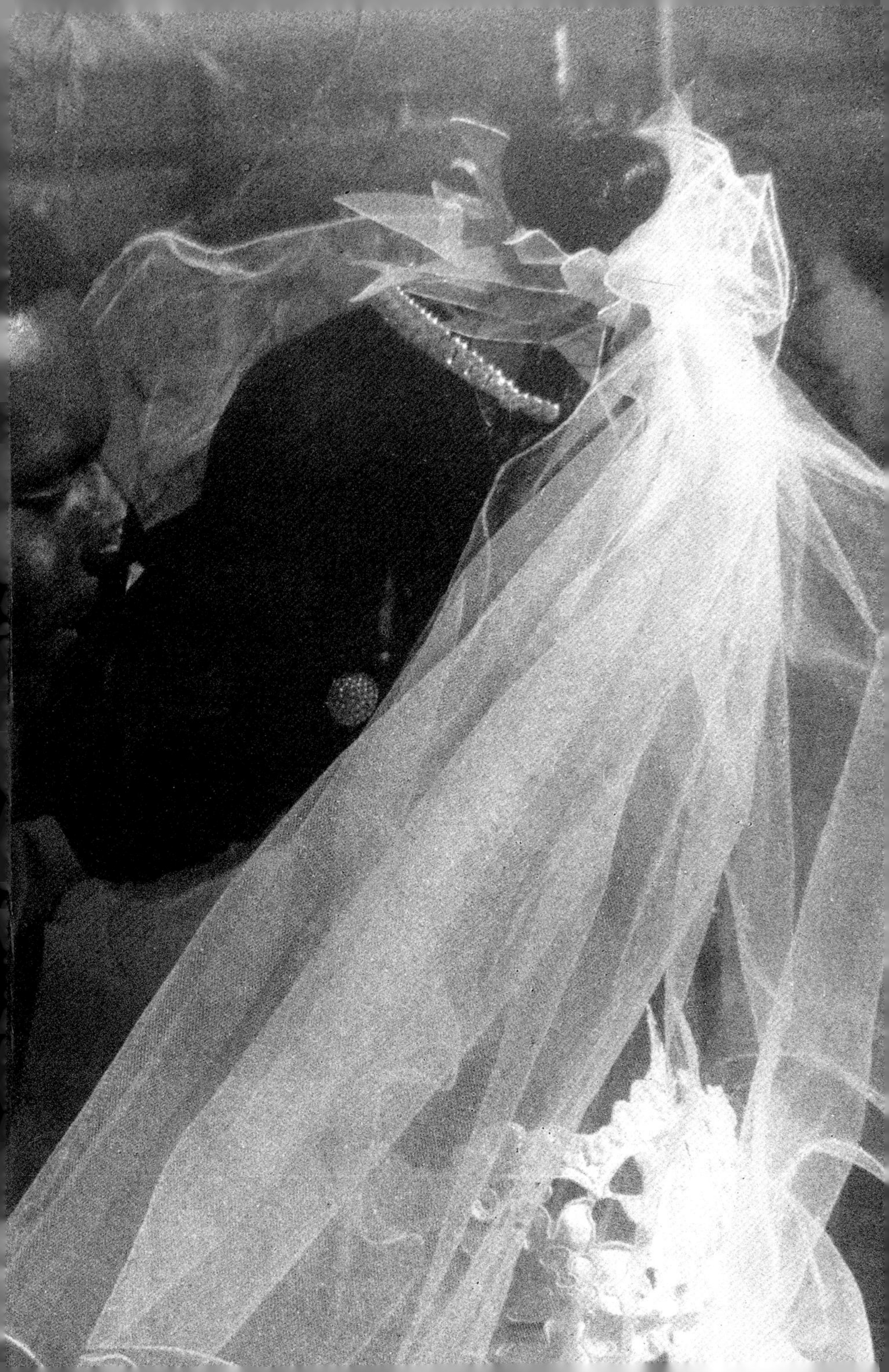

CREDITS

Courtesy of the artist and blank projects,
Cape Town © Sabelo Mlangeni 2022

All the illustrated works are hand-printed silver
gelatin prints, except for those listed below.

Silver gelatin print
p.20

C-print
p.41

Digital ultrachrome archival prints
pp.51, 53, 54, 61

ARTIST'S ACKNOWLEDGEMENTS

MY FAMILY AND FRIENDS
The Twelve Apolostolic Church of South Africa
    Ekuthuleni
The Christian New Stone Apostolic Church
Blank Projects team (Jonathan Garnham,
    Lemeeze Davis, Thobile Ndenze, Hannah Lewis,
    Catherine Humpries)
Antawan Byrd
Micheal Stevenson
Monique Du Blisses
Thiago de Paul Souza
Nkgopoleng Moloi
Dennis Da Silva
Andile Komani (LL Edition)
Tamar Garb
Kabelo Malatsie
Marie Ann Yemsi
Bisi Silva
Gabi Ngcobo
Umhlabathi Collective
Artur Walther
Marcedes Villarden
Sandra Philips
Ekow Eshun
Emmanuel Balogun
Joel Cabrita
Metthew S Witkovsky

EDITOR'S ACKNOWLEDGEMENTS

I would like to thank Sabelo Mlangeni for creating
an intimate and brave body of work, and for the good
humour he has shown throughout the entire process
of making this book together. I would also like to thank
Blank Projects in Cape Town, in particular Catherine
Humphries and Monique du Plessis.